MATHS IS NOT HOT
A COMEDIC JOURNEY TO ESCAPE MATHS AT SCHOOL

BY
BENJAMIN ANAFI-DE-KHEMS

All Rights Reserved © 2025 Benjamin Anarfi-De-Khems

No part of this publication may be reproduced, stored in a retrieval system, copied in any form or by any means, electronic, mechanical, photocopying, recording or otherwise transmitted without written permission from the publisher. You must not circulate this book in any format. Under no circumstances will any blame or legal responsibility be held against the publisher, or author, for any damages, reparation, or monetary loss due to the information contained within this book, either directly or indirectly.

For Penelope, Benjamin and Percival

Table Of Contents

Acknowledgement — V

Foreword — IX

Preface — XIII

Introduction — XVII

Chapter 1: The Plot — 1

Chapter 2: Jahman Vs Maths: The Ultimate Family Showdown — 9

Chapter 3: Maths: The Villain Nobody Asked For — 32

Chapter 4: A Plea For Freedom From Numerical Torment — 38

Chapter 5: Let's Talk About Dreams — 57

Chapter 6: Why Maths Lessons Miss The Mark For Jahman — 75

Chapter 7: Learning From The Best Around The World — 97

Chapter 8: The Journey To Find A Maths-Less Subject — 114

Chapter 9: From Coma To Clarity – Jahman's Maths Epiphany — 162

Bibliography — 205

Acknowledgement

First and foremost, I offer my deepest gratitude to the Lord God Almighty for His boundless grace, wisdom, and strength, which have carried me through this journey. Without His blessings, this book would still be just a funny idea floating in my head.

To my beloved partner, Dufie, and our amazing children—your unwavering love, patience, and encouragement have been my anchor (and occasional reality check). You stood by me through every twist and turn, cheered me on when the path got shaky, and reminded me that giving up was never an option. Your belief in me has powered every single page.

A heartfelt thank you to Mr. and Mrs. Kwame Osei Prempeh for your kindness, encouragement, and faith in my abilities. Your support has meant more than words can express.

To my incredible mum, Margaret Badu—your prayers, wisdom, and unconditional love have been the bedrock of my strength. Your faith in me has always spoken louder than my doubts, and for that, I'm eternally grateful.

A very special shout-out to Miss Colette Abimbola—thank you for seeing something special in my little story and saying, "This could be a book." That simple nudge (and your constant belief in my writing) helped bring this entire project to life. You helped me see the bigger picture—and I can't thank you enough.

Another shout-out to Mr. Everton Henry for designing the initial book cover—thank you for always stepping in with your creativity and support without hesitation. You're a legend.

Massive thanks to the entire Maths Department at Newman Catholic College—teachers and teaching assistants alike. Your dedication, humour, and camaraderie helped shape this book. Thank you for your passion, collaboration, and for surviving staff meetings with style.

Big appreciation to the London Book Publishers team for their amazing work in bringing this book to life. Your guidance, professionalism, and commitment have been invaluable.

To all my students—especially the unforgettable Class of 2022—this book wouldn't exist without your wild imaginations, hilarious logic, and unrelenting attempts to dodge maths. You've challenged me, inspired me, and reminded me why I love teaching (even when I'm marking your homework at midnight). Your questions sparked these pages, and your stories made them worth writing.

And finally, to everyone who supported, encouraged, or simply believed in me—thank you. Whether through kind words, helpful feedback, or a perfectly timed "You've got this," you've helped turn this dream into reality.

With deep appreciation and a sprinkle of humour.

Benjamin Anarfi-De-Khems

Foreword

Maths Is Not Hot is not your average maths book. It's not here to preach about long division or make you feel bad for forgetting your times tables. Instead, it's a laugh-out-loud, no-nonsense, sharply observant joyride through the twisted funhouse that is the British maths education system.

Picture this: a maths book with the rebellious spirit of a punk rock anthem, the nostalgia of a school reunion (minus the awkward small talk), and the wit of your funniest mate at the pub. That's what Benjamin delivers—a comedic battle cry for every student who's ever stared blankly at a whiteboard, every parent who's quietly Googled "What is a surd?", and every teacher who's wondered why the system still thinks copying from textbooks counts as "learning."

Benjamin dives headfirst into the trenches of our collective school memories, dragging up the horror stories of maths classes that felt more like psychological warfare than intellectual stimulation. He doesn't just tell jokes—he dissects the cultural, political, and institutional chaos that has turned UK maths education into something resembling an endurance test. All while students in countries like Estonia, Singapore, and South Korea are out here crushing it, sipping bubble tea and solving equations like it's a sport.

But don't get it twisted—this isn't some angry rant wrapped in fancy vocabulary. It's a playful, eye-opening story that laughs in the face of the "that's just how it's always been" mentality. With charm and irreverence, Benjamin reimagines maths as it *could* be: a space where creativity matters, collaboration is encouraged, and technology is a tool—not the enemy. Imagine a classroom where algebra makes sense, Pythagoras isn't a villain from your academic nightmares, and fractions don't induce an existential crisis. That's the dream. That's the revolution.

Importantly, *Maths Is Not Hot* isn't a textbook. It's not a teaching manual. It's not going to tell you how to run a classroom or structure a curriculum. What it *is*, is a storybook—yes, a funny, engaging, story-driven book about maths. One that sneaks in insights and truths about education, culture, and the global maths landscape while keeping you entertained. It's like learning by accident. The best kind.

If you're a student who hates maths, this book might just make you love it. If you're a teacher, it'll remind you why you started. If you're a parent, it'll give you hope. And if you're a policymaker... well, we hope you're taking notes, because this book does not hold back.

By the final chapter, you won't just understand the global maths crisis—you'll feel part of the solution. You'll laugh. You'll reflect. You might even find yourself reaching for a calculator *willingly*. And somehow, through the humour and chaos, *Maths Is Not Hot* might just make maths cool.

Who knew arithmetic could come with punchlines?

John Osei – Awuah

Gladesmore Community School

PREFACE

Let's be honest—if school subjects were celebrities, maths wouldn't be topping the charts. No one bursts through the classroom door yelling, "Yes! Algebra time!" Maths is more like that one party guest who kills the vibe by turning off the music to explain the history of long division while everyone else just wants to dance.

As a maths teacher, I've witnessed every creative escape attempt under the sun. Some students suddenly feel a profound, spiritual calling to reorganise their pencil case. Others take more "water breaks" than a marathon runner in the Sahara. And then there are the deep thinkers, staring dramatically into the middle distance like they're in a tragic indie film, silently willing the numbers to solve themselves. Of course, we can't forget the classic: "Sir, do I really need maths if I'm going to be a DJ?"

Honestly? I don't blame them. Maths has earned its reputation as the joyless villain of the timetable—dry, relentless, and wildly disconnected from actual life. So instead of preaching from the front of the classroom like a number-obsessed drill sergeant, I decided to flip the script. I wrote a story.

Not a textbook. Not a manual on how to survive quadratic equations. A proper story—something that makes you laugh like a great novel, while sneakily reminding you just how powerful maths can be.

This book is for the student who stares at a word problem like it's written in ancient hieroglyphics. For the one who breaks out in a cold sweat at the word "fractions." For anyone who's ever looked at a maths worksheet, sighed deeply, and thought, "Absolutely not."

At its heart, *Maths Is Not Hot* is about more than just dodging equations. It's about finding humour in the chaos, making peace with our shared classroom traumas, and maybe—even just a little—recognising that maths might be more useful (and more human) than we give it credit for.

So, is this book just here to drag maths through the mud? Not quite. Sure, it roasts maths a little. Okay, maybe a lot. But it also offers a fresh lens—a reminder that maths is hiding everywhere, whether you're splitting a bill, calculating a discount, or trying to figure out how little sleep you can get away with before work. You don't need to love numbers to enjoy this—you just need to be ready to laugh, reflect, and maybe rethink your relationship with maths.

And right now, that feels more urgent than ever. Across the globe, students are under pressure to "get" maths while battling boredom, anxiety, and the irresistible siren song of TikTok. Governments are rewriting curriculums, teachers are scrambling for solutions, and still the question lingers—how do we make maths feel human again? How do we make it *fun*?

This book is my answer. Part roast, part revelation, it's a slightly chaotic, deeply relatable, and surprisingly hopeful journey through the world of maths. So grab your sense of humour—and maybe a snack (because maths can be emotionally draining)—and let's dive into the madness. Spoiler alert: it's a lot more entertaining than you think.

Introduction

Mathematics. Just saying the word can make your palms sweat, bring on flashbacks of equations that felt like riddles from a maths-obsessed Sphinx, and trigger the eternal student lament: "When will I ever use this in real life?" No wonder 'Maths is not hot' resonates so deeply. But before we banish maths to the 'fun killer' corner, let's pause and rethink.

Here's a burning question for educators: should anyone get a free pass out of maths just because it's tough? What about those battling dyscalculia (which is essentially dyslexia only with numbers instead of words) or epic levels of maths anxiety—should they get a golden ticket out? And in any case, why do so many students flee from maths like it's a fire-breathing dragon? Is it because it feels as abstract as a Picasso painting? Or are the topics themselves—fractions, algebra, ratios, trigonometry, and circle theorems—about as relevant as learning how to milk a unicorn? Or maybe, just maybe, it's how we teach it.

So, what if we borrowed a trick or two from the global maths playbook? Singapore, China, Estonia—they've got maths education down to fine art. But here's the plot twist: maths isn't just important—it's secretly awesome. Yup, you heard me. And if you stick with me, I'll prove it.

Let's start with your daily life. Love gaming? Whether you're building pixel-perfect worlds, timing a leap of faith, or battling zombie hordes, maths is the wizard behind the curtain. It's in the graphics, the physics that make the game feel real, and the algorithms that adjust the difficulty to keep you hooked.

Not a gamer? Maybe you're more into TikTok or Instagram. Guess what? Maths powers every swipe, filter, trending challenge, and viral video. Likes, shares, and that oddly accurate 'For You' page? That's maths playing dress-up as an influencer.

And maths isn't done showing off yet. It's everywhere, hiding in plain sight. Your favourite sneakers? Thank Geometry for their killer design. That flawless batch of brownies? Fractions are baking up a storm. The GPS that saves you from getting lost? Trigonometry's your wingman. Maths is like the undercover superhero of our world—saving the day while staying humble.

But for that student who inspired this book, Jahman? Maths wasn't the hero. No, for him, maths was the ultimate nemesis—a relentless villain, always lurking, always waiting to pounce wherever he turned, numbers and equations were lurking like uninvited guests. So, Jahman launched a desperate mission: find a subject completely free of maths.

Is there a magical, maths-free paradise? Maybe another subject held the answer. Science?

Nope—calculations were baked into every experiment. Business studies? Surprise—percentages and profit margins made an appearance. Music? Beats, rhythms, and ratios jumped out like the bogeyman. Even art, my last refuge, betrayed me with symmetry and perspective.

"Is there anywhere I can escape this?" Poor old Jahman wondered.

Spoiler: there wasn't. Careers weren't safe either. Footballers calculate angles. Chefs measure ingredients. Even influencers—yes, influencers—are practically undercover mathematicians, analysing metrics and tweaking content strategies.

This book tells the story of my search, through Jahman's eyes, for a maths-free world. Another spoiler alert: neither Jahman nor I found one. But along the way, something wild happened.

Jahman realised that the problem wasn't maths itself; it was how he'd been looking at it.

So, buckle up for a journey through fractions, formulas, and more laughs than expected. By the end, you might just see maths for what it truly is: not just unavoidable, but maybe even… dare I say it… kinda cool. Let's dive in!

Chapter 1: The Plot

It was a sunny Friday afternoon during period five, and guess what the lesson was? Yup, Jahman's nemesis: Mr. Maths. Oh, the audacity of Mr. Head of Maths to slot such a torturous subject into period five—right after the class had spent lunch running around like maniacs playing football!

To say Jahman wasn't thrilled is an understatement. He was parched, exhausted, and already half-asleep. What could he do in that situation? Born into a family that's about as mathematically inclined as a colony of goldfish, he wasn't exactly Stephen Hawking or Nira Chamberlain material. His choices were clear: daydream or sleep. Today, daydreaming won.

Mr. Taribo West was at the front of the room, his voice animated, asking questions like "why?"

and "how?" and applauding answers like a motivational speaker. Jahman could tell the lesson was lively kids were engaged, hands were flying up, and the vibe in the room was surprisingly energetic. But Jahman? He was locked in his little bubble, waiting for that sweet bell to ring. The anticipation of Friday's jollof rice with jerk chicken, Mediterranean salad, and flaxseed was his sole source of comfort.

Mr. Taribo West knew better than to bother him on a Friday, especially during period five. He didn't even make eye contact, and Jahman appreciated his restraint. He understood the unspoken rule: don't poke the bear.

When the bell finally rang, Jahman didn't just leave—he bolted. Usain Bolt himself would've been jealous of his speed. Backpack slung over one shoulder; he flew out of that classroom with the energy of an Olympic sprinter. His mind was already halfway home, imagining the first bite of that glorious meal.

As he approached his house, he heard the unmistakable beat of Fuse ODG's 'Azonto' blasting from inside. The music was so loud he half-wondered if the family was hosting *Strictly Come Dancing*. There were screams, shouts, and what sounded like a full-on party. Jahman's heart skipped a beat. Had Grandad won the lottery?

The moment he walked through the door, the chaos reached a crescendo. Everyone turned to him, cheering like he'd just won the World Cup. "Congratulations, Jahman! That was stupendous!" his dad yelled, his face beaming with pride.

He froze. Him? Stupendous? Maths? There had to be some mistake. "Let me see my report, Dad," he said, skeptical. "I don't believe you."

Before Dad could respond, Grandmother chimed in, patting Jahman's shoulder. "Don't worry, my son. It was fabulous! You scored one out of 50."

"Wait. One out of 50?! What's that as a percentage?" Jahman asked, his voice cutting through the room like a last-minute goal in a heated derby.

The room fell as silent as the Emirates after Tottenham's stunning 3–2 comeback against Arsenal in November 2010. (Yes, Gooners, it happened. Let's move on.)

Then Jahman's dad, ever the mathematician in his own head, said: "I guess it's 10%. If you take the zero from the fifty and add it to the one, you get ten."

Bravo, Dad. Einstein would be *thrilled*.

Let's hit pause here. One out of 50 as a percentage is 10%? Really? Someone grab a calculator—or better yet, let's actually do the maths because 'take the zero and add it to the one' is not how percentages work. It's not how anything works.

Jahman blinked, confused. "But... why are you all celebrating?"

His mother, tears streaming down her face, stepped forward, her voice trembling. "Because my dear Jahman, you got one question correct this time. Remember, last term, you got zero! No one in this family has ever achieved such a fantastic result. We're so proud of you!"

Jahman stood there, flabbergasted. They were *jubilating* because he'd gone from zero to... one? His favourite song was blasting, his Asona family was dancing like maniacs, and suddenly, he was the golden child of the household.

And that's where the story begins. Believe it or not, Jahman is now officially the cleverest mathematician in his family, with a fabulous score of 2%. Can you believe that? Neither can I!

But before you judge, let's talk about where he came from.

The Asona family of Ashanti Mampong, part of the mighty Ashanti Kingdom, settled in the UK in the 1950s. A family with deep roots, rich traditions, and an ironclad work ethic. But also, a family plagued by one terrible, generational struggle: numbers.

Jahman's grandfather, Kwaku Duah, was a peasant farmer—a legend in the field. He could predict the rain like a human weather app, cultivate crops with military precision, and understand the seasons better than most scientists. But when it came to counting his maize? Chaos. A "double-check" often turned into a quadruple-check, and even then, he wasn't *entirely* sure if he had ten sacks or eleven.

His grandmother, Mama Akuah, was the glue of the family. She fed everyone, ran the household, and made sure things got *done*. But at the market? Let's just say some traders took one look at her maths skills and *smelled opportunity*. If a tomato seller told her five plus five was eleven, she just nodded and paid.

It wasn't just them. The struggle was real.

Jahman's father, Kuuku Dadzie, became a carpenter—a fantastic one, in fact. But measurements? His daily nemesis. A centimetre here, an inch there—sometimes, the furniture came out *just right*, and sometimes, the table wobbled like it had seen things.

His mother, Mama Dadzie, sold vegetables in the market. But giving change? Ah, that was an extreme sport. She would pause, count, pause again, count again, and then—*just in case*—look the customer dead in the eye and ask, "Are you sure this is correct?"

And then... *he* was born.

From the moment baby Jahman *failed to recognize numbers*, the family knew. They laughed and said he had inherited the dreaded "maths curse." It was in the blood, they declared. His teachers agreed—his *confused stare* at multiplication, his sheer **horror** at algebra, his ability to fail consistently and spectacularly.

It seemed his fate was sealed.

But could Jahman change it? Could he break the curse? Could he rewrite history and finally, finally, *finally* bring mathematical glory to the family?

Time will tell. Or maybe… the next test score will.

Chapter 2: Jahman Vs Maths: The Ultimate Family Showdown

Jahman stepped into the living room, already dreading the stack of maths homework waiting for him. Every day felt like a battlefield—him versus algebra, circle theorems, Pythagoras' theorem, percentages, ratios, and trigonometry. And the worst part? SOH CAH TOA. Those magical words his teacher chanted in class felt more like a spell to summon confusion. His stomach growled loudly. 'Borborygmi,' they called it in science, but it was just another distraction in maths.

"Maths is not hot," Jahman muttered under his breath. He couldn't help but hum Louis Armstrong's classic: *I see trees of green, red roses too... I see them bloom for me, and maths does too!* It was a tragic remix of a beautiful song, and he chuckled at the absurdity of it all.

At home, maths was about as welcome as Brussels sprouts at Christmas dinner—polite smiles on the surface, but everyone secretly wished it would disappear. The word *'percentage'* was strictly off-limits when discussing finances, as if saying it aloud might summon some mathematical demon. And circle theorems? Forget it. His parents wouldn't know the diameter of a hula hoop.

If Jahman even *whispered* "SOH CAH TOA," his mum would probably start Googling symptoms, while his dad would dial 999, convinced they were on the brink of a family-wide fainting emergency.

'Maths is definitely not hot,' Jahman thought, glaring at his homework as if it had just insulted his mum. Fractions loomed on the page like an ancient, unsolvable riddle from a cursed scroll. Adding them? Ha! About as likely as him winning the lottery. Drawing a straight line with a ruler?

Still a Herculean task—don't even *mention* triangles.

And yet his teacher expected him to conquer *trigonometry*—the mystical, cryptic realm of SOH CAH TOA. It felt less like a maths topic and more like some secret spell from a wizarding school he clearly hadn't been invited to.

In class, Jahman often walked in with a clean slate in his mind and left with an equally clean slate on his mini whiteboard. 'Maths is not hot,' he muttered during every lesson, a mantra of survival as he daydreamed about anything but numbers.

When his teacher asked him a question, his response was always the same: "I don't know." It wasn't laziness; it was honesty. Who could help him at home?

Mum

Jahman sat at the kitchen table, his maths book spread open like a crime scene, pencil tapping nervously against the page. Fractions, angles, and decimals stared back at him, mocking his every move. Desperate, he turned to his mum—the all-knowing oracle of wisdom, the superhero who could solve any problem. Surely she—his beacon of light and endless patience—could illuminate the murky abyss of his maths homework.

"Mum," he began, with the tone of someone asking for a life-saving potion, "do you know how to simplify fractions?"

She looked up from peeling vegetables, her expression softening. But then, to his surprise, she smiled and shook her head. "Oh, my dear," she said gently, "I don't know anything about maths."

Jahman blinked. "What? But why not? You know everything else!"

She set the knife down and wiped her hands on her apron, sitting across from him. "I wasn't allowed to go to school," she explained, her voice tinged with both pride and regret. "Your granddad was a peasant farmer, and your grandmum a housewife. There wasn't enough money to send me to school. I couldn't fulfil President Nelson Mandela's dream for peasant farmers—the one he spoke of in his priceless quote."

Jahman leaned forward, his curiosity piqued. "What quote, Mum?"

Her eyes gleamed as she recited the words, each syllable imbued with pride and longing:

"Education is the great engine of personal development. It is through education that the daughter of a peasant can become a doctor, that the son of a mine worker can become the head of the mine, and that a child of farm workers can become the president of a great nation."

Jahman sat back, letting the words sink in. "Wow, Mum," he murmured. "That's powerful."

She smiled and reached over to tousle his hair. "It is. And it's why I want you to study hard,

Jahman. Maths may be difficult, but every equation you solve is a step toward your dream."

Jahman nodded, feeling a renewed sense of determination. Maybe his mum couldn't help him with trigonometry, but she had given him something even better: inspiration.

"Thanks, Mum," he said, picking up his pencil. "I think I'll figure this out after all."

And as he bent over his workbook, he could almost hear President Mandela cheering him on.

Jahman's chest swelled with admiration. His mum, the strongest woman he knew, had never been taught how to solve for x, yet she solved a hundred daily problems with grace. 'Maths might not be her thing,' he thought, 'but she's the wisest person I know.'

Jahman stared at his maths homework, the numbers blurring together like a code he couldn't crack. With a deep breath, he decided to show it to his dad. If anyone could help, surely it was him.

Dad

"Dad," Jahman said, holding out his workbook, "can you help me with this maths problem?"

His dad looked up from his newspaper, raising an eyebrow. "Maths, huh?" He set the paper down and adjusted his glasses, giving the book a wary glance. "Alright, let's see what you've got."

Jahman watched hopefully as his dad studied the question. But then, with a heavy sigh, his dad leaned back in his chair. "You know, Jahman, I hate numbers. But I don't hate maths," he said, scratching his head thoughtfully.

Jahman frowned. "Wait... what? How can you hate numbers but not hate maths? Maths is all about numbers!"

His dad chuckled, ruffling Jahman's hair. "Exactly, kiddo. That's the problem. I like the logic and the problem-solving, but those pesky numbers always ruin it for me."

Jahman groaned, flopping onto the chair next to him. "So… that's a no, huh?"

His dad shrugged, smiling apologetically. "Sorry, son. Numbers and I don't get along too well. But hey, I believe in you. You've got this!"

Jahman shook his head, muttering under his breath as he picked up his pencil again. "Maths is not hot," he grumbled.

His dad laughed. "Nope, but it's useful. Good luck, champ!"

And with that, Jahman was back to square one, wondering if he'd ever find someone who could untangle the mysteries of maths.

Brother

Jahman stared at the maths worksheet in front of him, the numbers swimming on the page. He sighed and decided to call in reinforcements. His big brother was just a room away, lounging on the couch and fiddling with his Rubik's cube.

Big bro—the guy who could solve a Rubik's cube in under a minute and rattle off football stats like a human encyclopedia—surely he could help.

"Big bro, can you help me with this maths problem?" Jahman asked, his voice laced with hope.

His brother leaned back, smirking. "Me? Maths? Oh, no, no, no. I barely survived it myself. I think the calculator and I should've gotten a joint diploma."

Jahman's heart sank. Was this the same brother who could out-argue Mum on any topic and turn even the most boring story into a stand-up routine? Trigonometry was his kryptonite.

"Don't look at me like that," his brother laughed. "I can teach you how to nutmeg someone on the football pitch, but trigonometry? That's all you, buddy."

Jahman groaned. "Seriously? You're my last hope."

"Not in maths, I'm not," his brother said, shaking his head. "I hated it from primary school all the way to secondary. I only did the foundation GCSE paper, you know. Sorry, bro, I can't help."

Jahman blinked. "Wait, foundation? What's that?"

His brother's smirk widened. "Ah, let me enlighten you. In GCSE maths, there are two levels: foundation and higher. Both cover similar stuff, but the higher tier has all the scary advanced topics. Your teacher will probably suggest the foundation paper if you're not great at maths—or if you struggle, like me, Dad, or Auntie (but don't tell them I said that). It's easier."

"Easier, how?" Jahman asked, still not getting it.

"Well, the foundation paper caps at grade 5, which is still solid. But the higher paper? That's for the brainy types who want to do STEM stuff. It goes from grade 4 to 9, with 9 being the ultimate genius level."

"STEM? What's that?"

"Er, science technology, something and mathematics. Wait, I remember. Engineering."

"Right, right." Jahman squinted. "So… you took the foundation paper?"

His brother grinned sheepishly. "Yep. And proud of it. No shame, bro."

Jahman stared at him, deadpan. "Thanks, I guess. Is there a sub-foundation GCSE paper I can try?"

His brother burst out laughing. "Don't be silly. You'll figure it out. You're smarter than you think."

Jahman sighed as he turned away, muttering under his breath, "Smarter than you, apparently."

Auntie

Jahman tapped his pen against the edge of the table, staring at his untouched maths homework. After striking out with his brother, he decided to try a different route. Maybe Auntie would be the one to save the day. She was always full of stories and advice, and surely she could solve a simple maths problem. At least, he hoped it was simple.

"Auntie, can you help me with this maths question?" Jahman asked, hope flickering, albeit faintly, in his voice.

She glanced over, her face softening into a sympathetic smile. "Oh, Jahman, I didn't enjoy maths much either, my dear. Back in my day, I was taught by PE and Music teachers. Sorry, son."

Jahman froze, his brain grinding to a halt. "Wait... what? PE and Music teachers? Teaching maths? How does that even work?"

Auntie chuckled at his wide-eyed expression. "It was a different time, Jahman. Back then, maths specialist teachers were as rare as unicorns. Not many people studied maths at university, so schools had to make do with what they had. PE and Music teachers got 'volunteered' to teach maths because someone had to do it."

Jahman's jaw dropped. "You mean Mr. Whistle and Stopwatch were also solving equations? And Ms Guitar Strings was teaching Pythagoras?"

"Pretty much," said Auntie with a grin. "I remember one time our PE teacher tried to explain algebra while still wearing her netball bib. And the Music teacher? He once used a guitar chord diagram to explain angles."

Jahman shook his head, trying to picture it. "So, while other kids were learning maths from actual maths teachers, you were doing algebra with someone who could've been shouting, 'Drop and give me twenty!' or strumming chords in the background?"

"Exactly," Auntie said, laughing. "Even today, schools struggle to find enough maths specialists. That's why the UK government offers incentives and training programs to encourage people to become maths teachers. They're trying to fill the gaps left by the shortage."

Jahman sighed, leaning back in his chair. "So, you're saying your maths classes were taught by people who'd rather be doing warm-ups or playing ukuleles. No wonder maths wasn't your thing."

Auntie smiled knowingly. "Maths might not have been my favourite, but it doesn't mean it can't be yours, Jahman. Even if your teacher used to coach netball or play the ukulele, maths is still about how you approach it. Work at it, and you might even enjoy it."

Jahman groaned but couldn't help cracking a small smile. "Thanks, Auntie. But for the record, maths is still not hot."

"Not yet, Jahman," she said with a wink. "Not yet."

Uncle

Jahman slumped over his desk, staring at the problem that refused to solve itself. In a moment of pure desperation, he called in the big guns—his cool, collected, world-travelling uncle. Surely, the man who could tie a tie in ten different ways and always have a story for every situation could handle a little maths problem.

Jahman dialled the number and waited. When his uncle's deep, confident voice answered, he felt a spark of hope.

"Uncle!" Jahman exclaimed.

"Jahman, my boy! How's it going?"

"I need your help with my maths homework," Jahman admitted, his voice tinged with desperation.

"Maths? No problem, kid! What's the question?"

Jahman read it out carefully. "What is 30 minus 20 times 10 plus 40 divide by 10? BODMAS?"

For a moment, there was nothing but silence on the other end. Then, a dramatic gasp exploded through the phone, so loud that Jahman nearly dropped it.

"BOD-WHAT?!" his uncle bellowed, the sheer force of his confusion practically shaking the room.

Jahman winced, pulling the phone away from his ear. "Uncle? Are you okay?"

But there was no answer—just an eerie, otherworldly silence. Then, there was a strange whooshing sound out of nowhere, as if the universe had decided to fold in on his uncle.

"Uncle? Uncle!" Jahman called panic, creeping into his voice. He stared at the phone, half expecting his uncle to reappear with some profound explanation. Instead, there was only static.

Jahman blinked at the phone in disbelief. "Did BODMAS just… break him?" he muttered.

It was like the black hole of confusion had swallowed his uncle that maths always seemed to create. The man who could navigate foreign cities without a map and solve life's trickiest dilemmas had been defeated by a single maths problem.

That night, Jahman sat at his desk, staring at his unfinished homework. "Maths really isn't hot," he muttered, shaking his head.

And from that day on, Jahman never dared to bring up BODMAS with his uncle again.

Grandma

Jahman sighed, clutching his maths workbook as he shuffled into the living room. His last hope was sitting in her favourite armchair, knitting needles clicking away with the kind of precision that could only come from decades of experience. Surely Grandma—the family's wise matriarch who seemed to know everything—could help him.

"Grandma," Jahman began, approaching cautiously, "can you help me with this maths problem?"

She paused her knitting, squinting at him over her glasses. Her expression was a perfect blend of humour and tough love. "Oh, Jahman," she said, setting her knitting down, "I haven't been able to find x since 1966 England won the World Cup.

And now you want me to find y too? I'm afraid I can't do it, kid. Sorry!"

Jahman's jaw dropped. "But Grandma, you're always telling me, 'Knowledge is power!'"

She chuckled, patting his head. "Knowledge, yes. But maths? That's a whole different beast, my boy. I've been avoiding it since the hippie days, and I'm not about to start now."

Jahman groaned, slumping into the chair opposite her. "So, you're telling me maths isn't your thing either?"

"Not even close," she admitted with a wink. "I've made peace with it. That's why I let calculators do the heavy lifting. Besides, who needs fractions when you've got a good pie recipe?"

Jahman couldn't help but laugh, even as despair settled over him. If Grandma—who had lived through decades of victories, defeats, and the occasional World Cup win—couldn't conquer maths, what chance did he have?

He stood up, dragging his feet back toward his desk. "Maths has defeated my whole family," he muttered. "No wonder we leave it to the mathematicians."

Grandma called after him from her chair, "Cheer up, Jahman! Maths might not be hot, but at least you've got a family who can bake you a pie when you need a break!"

And for a moment, the weight of equations felt a little lighter.

Jahman slumped into his chair like a deflated balloon, staring hopelessly at the Everest-sized pile of maths homework looming on the table. *If my entire family is as mathematically gifted as a soggy biscuit,* he thought grimly, *surely there's another clan out there doing even worse.* His brain began to spiral, fast.

"Why can't the government just ban maths altogether? Or at least issue exemption cards to people like me—something like a Get-Out-of-Geometry-Free pass." He squinted at the ceiling dramatically. "They say 'Man shall not live by bread alone,' yeah? So who decided Pythagoras was part of a balanced diet?"

He glanced down at his workbook like it had personally offended him. "And who *is* this Mr. Maths anyway?" he muttered, jabbing his pencil against his forehead. "Does he think 'guinea pigs are actually pigs? Is he the same kind of genius who thinks Erling Haaland is a city in Scotland?"

His eyes narrowed. "Does Mr. Maths honestly believe just because everyone has ten fingers, we're all equally prepared to use them for long division? Or is he some sinister villain, lurking in the shadows, haunting generations of families like mine without consequence?"

Jahman sighed like he was carrying the weight of every failed maths test in human history. "And for the record," he added with a scowl, "just because my uncle's name is *Mathias* doesn't mean I'm genetically gifted at maths. My whole family has about as much in common with Nira Chamberlain as a fish does with a Wi-Fi password."

He glared at the question in front of him: *If Train A leaves the station at 60 mph and Train B leaves at 80 mph...*

"Who. Actually. Cares?" he muttered, dragging his hand down his face. "Do I look like someone preparing for a career in theoretical rail logistics? I'm not trying to be a mathematician—or worse, a numerologist!"

His pencil waved through the air like a sword of defiance. "And what's with his creepy extended family?" Jahman continued, clearly on a roll. "Numbers, always sneaking around like they've got something to hide. Then there's his mysterious cousin, *Numeracy*—everyone talks about him, but no one really knows what he does. And don't even get me started on that annoying American nephew, *Math*—the guy couldn't even keep the 's'. How rude is that?"

He leaned back in his chair, cracked his knuckles, and took a deep breath. "Alright then," he declared to no one in particular. "Let's dive into this weird little number cult and see what they're really about."

Because sometimes, even when you're being emotionally assaulted by algebra, all you can do is channel your inner drama king and prepare for battle.

Chapter 3: Maths: The Villain Nobody Asked For

Jahman's mind spun like a fidget spinner on turbo speed, trying to untangle the endless confusion between Math, Maths, Mathematics, Numeracy, and Numbers. "Why are there so many names for the same tormenting subject?" he groaned. "Are they trying to confuse us further? It's like a bad boy band that keeps changing their name to stay relevant—'Introducing: Numeracy and the Fractions!' or 'The Geometry: Live in Concert!'" Jahman snorted. "No amount of rebranding will make this subject cool. Maths is not hot."

He slumped in his chair, shaking his head. "Why the numerous options?" Jahman muttered to himself. "In America, it's just *Math*—short and sweet, like ripping off a Band-Aid. But cross the pond to the UK, and suddenly it's *Maths* like adding an extra *s* makes it any better. And then there's *Mathematics,* which sounds like the evil boss of the whole operation, complete with a cape and a sinister laugh. Oh, and don't forget *Numeracy.* Is that Maths' polished cousin who went to finishing school and speaks in decimals instead of sentences?" Lurking in the corner is Arithmetic**,** the grumpy grandad of the bunch— the old-school disciplinarian who yells, *'Back in my day, we didn't have calculators! We carried the one with our bare hands!'*

Jahman threw up his hands. **"It's exhausting! At this point, just call it Traumatis-tics and be done with it!"**

He started pacing up and down the room. "It's like they're deliberately multiplying their names to intimidate us. I half-expect to see *Mathology* trending one day as the next big thing. Whatever they call it, it's still the same dreadful subject, ambushing me with percentages, square roots, and the dreaded *x*. And let's face it," he added, "according to my grandma, *x* has never been found. Maths is like a bad remake of a movie no one wanted—no matter how you package it, it's still a flop."

Jahman paused, scratching his head. "Alright, let's start with the big question: What even *is* mathematics? Is it just numbers doing acrobatics on a page? A fancy name for solving problems that make your brain hurt? Or maybe it's some ancient sorcery magicians disguised as mathematicians used to explain the universe?"

He frowned, deep in thought. "People throw around terms like 'math' and 'mathematics,' but what are we discussing? A universal language? A puzzle master's toolkit? Or just cleverly disguised mental torture that schools decided to endorse?" Jahman sighed. "Let's dig in and find out."

To Jahman's broccoli-shaped brain, mathematics felt like the ultimate villain in a superhero movie—a cunning mastermind with an arsenal of endless equations, devious theorems, and a diabolical plan to baffle every innocent mind. "It's a villain," Jahman said dramatically, "with an army of numbers and symbols striking fear across the world." He imagined a dark figure looming over the globe, raining down algebraic expressions and quadratic traps. "If there were an Avengers team to save us, I'm pretty sure Iron Man would take one look at trigonometry and say, 'Nope, I'm out!'"

He continued, "And then there's *Numeracy,* which sounds like wizardry from a fantasy novel. Is it a spell wizard chant to summon numbers? I can almost picture it now: 'Numerous Revealicus!'" He waved his hands theatrically. "Suddenly, glowing fractions, menacing decimals, and swirling percentages fill the room like magical runes of doom."

Jahman shuddered. "If that's Numeracy, count me out. I didn't sign up for the Hogwarts School of Mathematical Sorcery. I'm no wizard, and the last thing I need is accidentally summoning a frequency polygon that follows me around like a cursed ghost." He chuckled to himself. "Can you imagine trying to live with irrational roots whispering probabilities in your ear? No thanks. Numeracy might sound mystical, but I'd rather stick to charms and potions that don't involve calculating the area of a circle."

He paused, mulling it over. "Do I even need maths to be an Uber driver? I know how to drive, and the app does all the calculating for me... right?"

Suddenly, an idea struck him like lightning. "This is it!" Jahman exclaimed, eyes gleaming. In a burst of dramatic inspiration, he grabbed his phone and fired off a tweet:

Petition to ban Maths from schools and replace it with 'How to Survive Life 101.' Who's with me?!

And so, the battle raged on—Jahman versus Maths—an epic struggle that would go down in family history. The quest for freedom from numbers had begun, and Jahman wasn't backing down without a fight.

Chapter 4: A Plea for Freedom from Numerical Torment

Jahman is absolutely done with this relentless mathematical torment. Every fibre of Jahman's being screams in protest, but the numbers keep coming. Maths feels less like a school subject and more like an ancient curse passed down through generations to haunt the unsuspecting. Jahman thinks his hatred for maths started before he was born. He can almost picture Baby Jahman in the womb, flinching as the doctor counted heartbeats, thinking, 'Seriously, Doc? Must we quantify every vibe?'

From the very beginning, maths and Jahman have been locked in a bitter feud. It's not just a villain; it's his lifelong nemesis, popping up in every corner of his life like a bad sequel no one asked for. It's the clingy antagonist that refuses to

Maths Is Not Hot

leave the story, always there, lurking in the background.

Maths is like that overly persistent friend who insists on tagging along, even after Jahman has made it painfully clear they're not invited. "Mr. Education Secretary," Jahman pleads, "please, let Maths crash someone else's party!"

And it's not just Jahman. Mathematical incompetence is practically a family tradition. His parents? Helpless. His grandparents? Completely clueless. His cousins? Don't even ask. Even his dog avoids him when he pulls out a calculator. It's as if their DNA is encoded with biscuit cravings and an uncanny ability to lose the TV remote but absolutely no mathematical aptitude. The family's crowning achievement in maths? Timing the kettle to boil during the ad break.

Despite this glaring evidence of inherited hopelessness, the Department for Education insists on cramming maths into Jahman's brain like an intellectual superfood. Fractions, algebra, surface area, stem and leaf keep piling it on, hoping that one day Jahman will wake up and say, "Oh wow, division is delightful!" Spoiler alert: that's never happening. No app, colourful textbook, or chirpy video tutorial will ever make long division charming.

What's the grand plan here? Do they think if they shove enough equations Jahman's way, he'll miraculously transform into a human calculator? Or will Pythagoras descend from the heavens to show him the spiritual beauty of triangles? Because let Jahman tell you—it's not working. Instead, he's convinced maths belongs in the same category as slow wi-fi and soggy fries: universally disliked, and for good reason.

A gold star excuse

But wait—aha! Jahman's got the ultimate, gold-star excuse, and it's practically unchallengeable: he's autistic, he's got ADHD, he's grappling with maths anxiety, and let's not forget his lifelong arch-nemesis—dyscalculia. That's right, folks—he's an official card-carrying member of the SEND (Special Educational Needs and Disabilities) squad. Surely, with this superhero lineup of barriers, the universe itself is shouting, "Give this kid a maths-free pass already!" Come on, Mr. Headteacher, doesn't this scream, "Let's spare Jahman from the Pythagorean nightmares"?

Let's break it down, shall we? Maths anxiety isn't just disliking numbers. Oh no—it's a full-blown fight-or-flight response. Think sweaty palms, heart racing, and a brain freeze so icy it could stop global warming. Someone casually asks, "What's 7 times 8?" and Jahman's inner voice screams, "Abort mission!" It's a fear so paralyzing it makes long division feel like jumping out of a plane without a parachute.

Then there's dyscalculia, Jahman's long-time frenemy. Numbers? They're like that confusing friend who never texts back and keeps switching personalities. A 6? Looks like a 9. Decimals? Just commas in a fake mousetache. It's a maths circus, and poor Jahman is the reluctant ringmaster trying to keep it all together.

ADHD? Forget focusing on a single maths problem for longer than two minutes. It's like trying to read *War and Peace* in the middle of a dance party. And autism? Jahman has a very curated list of obsessions—and believe it or not, quadratic equations didn't make the cut.

With all these challenges, isn't it obvious? Asking Jahman to survive a maths lesson is like asking a goldfish to scale Mount Everest. It's not just unreasonable—it's downright cruel. So, yeah, maths? It's still not hot. Not even a little.

So, Mr. Headteacher, Jahman is begging you: throw him a lifeline here. You've got the power to save him from a lifetime of endless fractions and indecipherable graphs. Why not grant him a special dispensation? A maths-free life would mean he could finally focus on things he's actually good at—like dodging numbers, writing witty complaints about maths, or figuring out how to escape mandatory lessons entirely.

Surely, this has to be the ultimate loophole, right? A legal, ethical, and moral reason to banish maths from his life for good? Come on, let's do everyone a favour and make this happen. Jahman will even frame your decision as groundbreaking: 'The day a Headteacher saved a student from the tyranny of maths.' Sounds like a good headline, doesn't it? He'll even add a dedication in his future autobiography. So, what do you say? Maths is not hot, and Jahman is the living proof.

Can anyone out there hear Jahman's cries of desperation? Jahman is done with this maths nonsense. We hate maths! It's not just a dislike—

it's a full-blown revolt. We don't understand it or like it, and honestly, most of us are as lost in maths lessons as a fish trying to climb a tree. Sitting in those classes feels like being sucked into a black hole—one that devours our confidence, sanity, and will to live. Numbers swirl around us, equations loom like storm clouds, and just when you think you've got a grip on fractions, along comes algebra to throw you back into chaos. Maths is not hot!

Please, Jahman is begging—let's banish maths from the curriculum forever. Imagine the joy, the sheer relief, if future generations could live in a world where no one ever had to ask, 'If Train A leaves the station at 2 p.m. and Train B leaves at 3 p.m., when will they meet?' No more probability tree diagrams, no more soul-crushing word problems, no more staring at a page full of numbers that might as well be scribbles.

Honestly, isn't it time someone listened to us? We're sitting in those classrooms, drowning in decimals and lost in polygons. We're waving our metaphorical white flags, shouting, "We surrender!" But instead of help, they just throw more worksheets at us. Enough is enough. Maths might be hot for some, but for us? Maths is not hot. It's the opposite of hot—it's ice-cold misery, and it's time to let it go. Forever.

Mr Lennox Lewis

Should Jahman grab his cape, channel his inner superhero, and single-handedly banish maths from secondary schools forever? Whoa, hold your horses! Jahman's no vigilante—he knows this mission calls for a professional. Someone with power, precision, and a record of delivering devastating knockouts.

Enter the one and only Mr Lennox Lewis, the undisputed heavyweight champion of the world and Jahman's secret weapon. If anyone can step into the ring and deliver a one-two combo to fractions, algebra, and their pesky gang of formulas, it's him.

"Alright, Maths," Jahman smirks, imagining Lennox in his corner. "Your days are numbered. And trust me, they're not looking too hot. Mr. Lennox Lewis, could you do us all a favour and step into the ring on our behalf? Picture it: Maths personified, standing there smugly with its confusing fractions, infuriating decimals, and smug algebraic proofs. And then—boom! —you land one of your famous uppercuts, sending algebra flying out of the ring. Imagine the roar of the crowd as you deliver a right hook to simultaneous equations, a jab to surface area of 3D shapes, and a finishing blow to trigonometry!

"You've knocked out giants before, Mr Lewis, so surely estimating mean and reverse percentages are no match for you. And don't worry about angles and vectors; we'll leave those calculations to the commentators. This could be the fight of the century: Lennox Lewis vs Maths, live from every classroom around the world."

With one final knockout punch, maths would be sprawled on the canvas, the referee declaring, "Maths is officially down for the count!" You'll go down in history as the champion who finally freed students everywhere from the tyranny of equations. And Jahman? He'll be the ecstatic fan in the front row, chanting, "Maths is not hot!"

Surds everywhere

People love to call maths the 'universal language', proudly claiming that the same numbers and symbols are used in every country. But honestly, is that really a flex? Jahman means, just because it's everywhere doesn't make it welcome. Whether you're strolling through the legendary Diego Armando Maradona's beloved Argentina or trekking to the late great President Mugabe's Zimbabwe, maths is lurking like a determined stalker, ready to ambush you with algebra, geometry, or—wait for it—a surd.

Did Jahman say 'Surd'? Yes, he did. What sort of creature is a surd anyway? A mythical beast? A cryptid? It sounds like something Indiana Jones would be searching for: 'The Curse of the Lost Surd.' Jahman can already see the movie poster now! But alas, it's just another one of Maths' strange, intimidating concepts designed to confuse us mortals.

Maths is like that annoying tourist who insists on photobombing every picture you take, no matter where you go. Standing in front of the Eiffel Tower? Bam—Maths is in the background. Posing by the Great Wall of China? There it is again, grinning smugly with its pi symbols and graphs. When ordering pizza, maths also pops up, dividing the slices into fractions. You can try to ignore maths, but never underestimate it wherever it comes, lol.

Jahman thinks, 'If maths were a person, it'd be that guy who shows up uninvited to every party and stands in the corner with a pocket protector, talking about prime numbers while everyone else is trying to have a good time.' Honestly, Jahman's never heard of a mathematician becoming the president of any country. Barack Obama didn't need to know the Pythagorean theorem to get elected, did he? So why does Jahman need to be a genius at fractions to make it in life? Jahman's role model, Richard Branson, isn't a mathematician, and he's a billionaire! And Michael Jackson? The King of Pop didn't use algebra to write his legendary music. He didn't solve for x to create 'Thriller' or 'Billie Jean.'

These legends didn't rely on maths to reach the top of their fields. So why should Jahman let solving equations and frequency polygons stand in the way of his future? Should he be focusing on memorising formulas, or should he be out there, dancing like MJ or making game-changing moves like Richard Branson? The answer seems obvious.

Maths isn't hot, and frankly, Jahman would rather be the next pop icon or successful entrepreneur than the world's next mathematician.

What practical use does adding or subtracting fractions have in daily life? When was the last time Jahman sat down with a pizza and thought, 'Hmm, I need to add 3/8 of a slice to 5/16 of a slice to figure out how much pizza I have left'? Never. Does Jahman need geometry to succeed as a businessman buying and selling cars? Unless he's designing a car from scratch, he doubts it. All Jahman needs to know is the price tag and engine size—that's more than enough for him!

Will knowing Pythagoras' theorem help Jahman operate the till at Tesco? Highly unlikely. No one at the checkout is going to ask, "Could you solve for x before I ring up your groceries?" Imagine walking into Tesco and declaring, "I'll pay for this milk once I calculate the square root of the store floor space!" Jahman's pretty sure he'd be escorted out by security. Maths just doesn't seem essential for the real-world situations he'll face.

If Jahman was trying to make a sale, the last thing on his mind would be the hypotenuse of a triangle. He'd be focused on connecting with customers, understanding what makes cars run smoothly, and knowing when to haggle. Maths? Not so much. It doesn't feel relevant to the practical skills he needs to thrive—like communication, creativity, and problem-solving in real-life scenarios.

Maths is not hot. It doesn't have that spark, that excitement, or that 'cool factor' like the latest tech gadgets, entrepreneurial success stories, or even mastering a TikTok dance. Give Jahman real-world skills over numbers any day. Maths is just not the star of the show in the life he's trying to create.

Why can't we just leave it behind, like lost luggage at Accra airport Terminal 3? Imagine the relief: "Ladies and gentlemen, your plane is ready for boarding—don't worry, maths didn't make it through security." Now, that's the kind of universal language Jahman would subscribe to. Let's be honest—Maths is not hot.

For the love of humanity, can we please just show maths the door? Politely, of course. "Thanks for coming, but we've got enough chaos without you turning the piñata into a geometry lesson." Imagine the collective sigh of relief as we all get back to enjoying life without decimal points raining on our parade. Life's party would be so much better without it.

Jahman's not training to be a rocket scientist or an astrophysicist. The only stars he's interested in are on Netflix or TikTok. Yet, he is wrestling with Venn diagrams and sequences like his future depends on them. Free him, he begs you! Let him live life blissfully untouched by similar triangles or the haunting spectre of x.

And then there's Jahman, who always says, "Bro, you think maths is tough? You've gotta learn how to dodge these numbers like a pro. The world's waiting for you to drop your next TikTok dance, not your next equation." He's not wrong. While Jahman's grappling with fractions, his mates are mastering new moves for their latest videos. He gets it.

And let's not forget the 'calculator generation.' With a smartphone in his pocket, Jahman's one app away from solving any maths problem that life dares to throw at him. Need to split a restaurant bill? There's an app for that. Want to calculate your mortgage payments? Google's got him covered. It's like maths outsourced itself to technology and forgot to tell us, "Hey, relax. I've got this!" Why wrestle with long division when Siri or Alexa can do it faster, cleaner, and with zero stress?

Jahman's motto is simple: Why stress over numbers when your phone can do all the heavy lifting? It's 2025, fam, not 1825. That's why he's all in on this—no need to get caught up in the maze of maths when technology's got our backs.

Picture this: a world without maths. Numbers would exist purely as decorative sprinkles on cupcakes, not the monstrous battles we're forced into at school. Why can't Jahman join this numerical utopia? Let mathematicians keep their calculators and graphs; he'll stick to rounding up spare change at the corner shop. Jahman says, "Bro, even cavemen didn't need trigonometry. They had fire, caves, and no stress." He's right. Cavemen didn't need trigonometry to survive in the jungle, however; they invented fire, painted on walls, and survived sabre-tooth tigers.

So here he is, waving the white flag of surrender. Jahman doesn't want to calculate angles, draw cumulative graphs, or work out ratios. His brain simply wasn't designed for numerical gymnastics. He'll leave that to the pros—he's got the moves, and Jahman's got the complaints.

Grab your popcorn, folks, because the saga of *Jahman vs Maths* is about to get juicier than a Netflix drama. Forget cliffhangers—this is the real deal. Jahman's journey through the labyrinth of numbers, equations, and formulas is the kind of story that deserves its own movie trailer. Imagine an intense voiceover:

In a world where numbers rule… one man dares to defy the tyranny of algebra. Coming soon: 'Maths is Not Hot: The Jahman Chronicles.'

But let's cut to the chase—why does Jahman think maths is colder than yesterday's leftover pizza?

Let's break it down in the next chapter of this thrilling tale.

Chapter 5: Let's Talk About Dreams

Uber

When Jahman grows up, he wants to be an Uber driver—cruising around town with his playlist blasting, passengers enjoying his five-star customer service, and Google Maps handling the directions. The app will calculate the fare faster than anyone can say 'surge pricing.' So tell us, Mr. Head of Maths, why must Jahman endure this endless torture of algebraic equations and SOH CAH TOA nightmares on earth?

And Jahman just shakes his head and says, "Fam, if you think maths is tough, wait until you're dodging numbers out in the real world. Ain't no Uber ride worth taking if you don't know how to hustle." Jahman's got a point: he can't see why anyone would need to solve for x when there's a perfectly good app. He's all about real-world smarts: "Forget quadratic equations, bro. Let's talk shortcuts and how to avoid traffic!"

Is there some secret Uber crash course where trigonometry is a prerequisite? Will Jahman need to solve for x one day to find the shortest route to pick up Mr OFSTED? Because if that's the case, he missed the memo. No passenger has ever leaned forward and said, "Excuse me, but before we go, could you calculate the angle of this ridiculously sharp turn?"

The only angles Jahman cares about are the ones on Google Maps, and guess what? The app does all the thinking for him. As he'd say: "You want angles? Check the GPS, but don't come at me with triangles. Maths is not hot."

And what about percentages? The app handles splitting fares, calculating tips, and applying discounts. There's no need for Jahman to whip out a calculator mid-ride to figure out how much of his fee goes to Uber. So, Mr Maths, isn't it time to admit that all this extra stuff is overkill? What's next? Can we use quadratic equations to parallel park? Jahman would laugh and say: "Nah, fam. Just park like a boss and leave the maths to the textbooks. Ain't no need for calculus in a parking space."

Maths might be great for engineers, scientists, and astronauts, but for an Uber driver like Jahman? It's about as useful as a flat tire. So please, Mr Head of Maths, set him free. Let Jahman focus on what really matters: memorising shortcuts, discovering the best late-night kebab spots for passengers and delivering that legendary five-star service. No trigonometry is required. As Jahman would say: "Just get me to my destination, keep the vibes high, and leave the maths out of it, bro."

All Jahman wants is to be an Uber driver when he grows up. Can someone please explain why ferrying people from point A to point B requires him to conquer ratios or expand double brackets? He doesn't want to calculate the volume of a cylinder—he just wants to drive! Let him focus on the maths that matters: figuring out how many pizzas are needed to order for a movie night or making sure he has enough coins for the bus. That's his happy place—simple, practical, and stress-free.

He doesn't need to calculate the velocity of his car while picking up passengers, or stress about the exact area of a triangle when he should be dodging traffic. Seriously, what's more important? The area of a triangle or avoiding a pothole?

Anything beyond that? Sorry, Maths, but you're just not Jahman's vibe. He's not about those complicated formulas. He's about trying to figure out the best route to avoid rush hour. You want him to solve for x? Jahman says, "Nah, I'm just trying to avoid traffic jams, not algebraic nightmares!"

The United Nations

And, Mr Prime Minister, while I've got your attention, let me drop a little food for thought. My friend Kofi Annan dreams of becoming the Secretary-General of the United Nations. A big dream, right? But here's the thing—do you think that job involves solving simultaneous equations or calculating the volume of a triangular prism? I highly doubt Kofi will ever need to sit in a meeting and say, "Hold on, folks, let me calculate the area of this triangle before we address world peace." So why should Kofi waste precious hours of his life wrestling with the quadratic formula when he could be learning about diplomacy, global politics, or, you know, saving the planet?

Papa on stage

Now, let me tell you about my mate Papa. The guy's got big plans—he wants to be the next big thing in the music world. A star on stage, with crowds screaming his name. But, Mr Prime Minister, do you think Papa will ever need to solve for x to write his next hit song? Nah. He's too busy figuring out the perfect beat, crafting lyrics, and ensuring his music video goes viral. I'm pretty sure there's no chorus about quadratic equations in his next track. Papa would be like, "Yo, Mr. Prime Minister, I'll leave the maths to you while I focus on these tracks. Let's get it!"

Member of Parliament

And while we're on the subject, let's talk about my cousin, Kwasi Kwarteng. The guy wants to become an MP—a respectable ambition if there ever was one. But tell me, Mr Prime Minister, does being an MP require algebra? Is he expected to calculate the gradient of a line while debating housing policies? Unless the House of Commons has some secret committee dedicated to plotting bar charts and solving linear inequalities, I think it's safe to say that Kwasi can safely skip maths. His time would be much better spent mastering public speaking, writing compelling speeches, and shaking hands at local events—not memorising Pythagoras' theorem.

Unless you can prove that MPs are out here solving quadratic inequalities to pass legislation, can we all agree that Maths has no place in Kwasi's political training? Let the guy focus on the real challenges of politics—like how to smile during awkward photo ops and avoid scandal. Jahman would probably say, "Kwasi, don't waste your time on maths—just keep hustling and making those moves!" Maybe that could even be a plank on which to campaign for election: Maths is not hot!

So please, Mr Prime Minister, give Kofi, Kwasi, and Papa the chance to focus on their real dreams instead of being chained to the never-ending misery of Maths. Redirect their energy toward meaningful skills, not mental gymnastics over Thales of Miletus circle theorems. Let them thrive, and more importantly, let the rest of us off the hook while you're at it. Jahman would give a thumbs-up to that.

Modelling

Oh, Mr Minister of Education, I just had a sudden realisation! My next-door neighbour, Afia (she was born on a Friday), a lovely and ambitious girl, has her sights set on becoming the next Naomi Campbell. Yes, you heard that right—she dreams of strutting down runways, rocking the latest fashion trends, and catwalking around the world to applause and flashing cameras. But here's the burning question: does she really need to know cubic functions for that?

I mean, think about it—when was the last time Naomi stopped mid-strut to factorise a quadratic expression or used trigonometry to adjust her angle on the runway? Never! The only angles models worry about are camera angles, and the closest thing they get to a 'cubic' is the cubicle-sized changing rooms backstage at Fashion Week.

So, Mr Minister of Education, can Afia be exempted from doing Maths? Surely her time would be better spent practising her poses, working on her walk, or figuring out how to smile without actually smiling (a true modelling skill). Unless cubic functions are somehow involved in calculating the height of her heels or the length of her catwalk stride… well, is there any connection?

Let's be practical here. The modelling world already has enough numbers—dress sizes, shoe sizes, and maybe an occasional runway measurement. But cubic functions? Let's leave those for the engineers and scientists. So please, Mr Head of Maths, let Afia off the hook and let her focus on living her catwalk dreams. Maths might be hot for architects and mathematicians but for the next Naomi Campbell?

Football

Once again, Mr Headteacher, we've got a situation that demands your immediate attention! Kojo, the boy with stars in his eyes and a football permanently glued to his feet, dreams of becoming the next Cristiano Ronaldo, the maestro of the pitch, the man who turns football into poetry. But here's the question we all need to ask: does drawing histograms or sine graphs have anything to do with scoring goals? Spoiler alert: they don't. Kojo doesn't need to know how to plot a frequency polygon to perfect his free kick. He's not calculating the angle of a sine curve when he launches the ball into the top corner with a jaw-dropping bicycle kick. No referee has ever paused a game to say, "Kojo, before you take that penalty, can you sketch a histogram of your shooting success rate this season?"

If Kojo had Jahman's mindset, he'd be focused on mastering his footwork, getting his ball control sharp, and working on his game-winning moves—not sitting in class drawing graphs. Let's be realistic here. Kojo needs time to train, practice his footwork, and fine-tune his celebration dance for when he scores that match-winning goal in the Champions League final. Histograms? He can leave those to the statisticians analysing his performance on Sky Sports. Sine graphs? Maybe they'll come in handy if he ever needs to calculate the curve of a banana shot, but let's face it—his instinct and hours of practice will do the job just fine.

So, Mr Headteacher, let's cut Kojo some slack and let him focus on what matters: becoming the next GOAT. Free him from the shackles of angles and axes, and let him shine on the pitch. Cristiano Ronaldo didn't get to where he is by mastering pie charts, and Kojo won't either. Jahman would tell you the same—Kojo's got the skills to pay the bills, not the simultaneous equations. Let's send him off to conquer the footballing world, where the only numbers he needs to worry about are the ones on the scoreboard. Maths is not hot for future footballing legends!

Even experts struggle with maths—so why should Jahman bother?

Why is it that dads, mums, uncles, aunties, and even grandparents love to boast about how they were hopeless at maths back in the day, but you never hear them say the same about English? Have you ever heard anyone proudly declare, "I was terrible at spelling and didn't know what a noun was until I was thirty"? Nope. But mention fractions, and suddenly everyone's got a horror story to share, as if surviving maths deserves some kind of war medal.

Enter Jahman, sitting there thinking, 'Okay, so we're all supposed to suck at maths? Great. But why does that feel like a badge of honour?' Jahman's got a point—maybe it's because maths always feels like it's out to get you. English lets you wiggle your way out of a tough spot. If you don't know the exact meaning of a word, you can just make something up that sounds halfway decent. Write a poem that doesn't rhyme. No problem—it's 'abstract.' Maths, on the other hand, is like that no-nonsense drill sergeant who demands precision. Either your answer is right, or it's wrong. No gold star for trying. No 'creative interpretation' for 2 + 2 = 5.

Jahman's had enough of this strict maths vibe. He says, "Maths is like the strict headteacher who makes you sit up straight and follow the rules, while English is the cool art teacher who says, 'Express yourself!' Maths says, 'Show your working,' while English says, 'Show your feelings.'" No wonder maths gets blamed for everything from bad report cards to sleepless nights. English gets to wear the cool leather jacket, while maths is stuck in a stiff suit with a calculator sticking out of its pocket.

And it's not just students who feel this way. Have you noticed how grown-ups—even the so-called 'experts'—talk about maths? You've got headteachers, professors, doctors, and even TV personalities admitting they struggled with it. They'll laugh about it, like it's some kind of shared secret. "Oh, I couldn't do algebra to save my life," they say with a chuckle, as if that's totally fine. But can you imagine one of them saying, "I never really got the hang of reading"? They'd be booed off the stage!

Jahman's thinking, 'Wait a minute, why should I sit here, sweating over a page of numbers, struggling silently with maths when even the so-called experts freely admit they weren't great at it in school? These are the people running companies, saving lives, and hosting quiz shows, yet they're out here casually confessing that algebra once made them cry. If they couldn't conquer it, why should I even bother? What's the point of stressing over decimals and fractions when the real world seems to be getting along just fine without them?'

Jahman pauses, then says, "Think about it. Is maths really essential for survival? Are there packs of wild mathematicians roaming the streets, ready to pounce on anyone who can't recite their timetables? Probably not. Can't I just get by with instincts, common sense, and maybe a decent calculator app? After all, life is full of tools and shortcuts—surely I don't need to calculate angles to find my way around. Google Maps has me covered, right?"

And honestly, how often do people actually use the maths they learned in school? Jahman laughs to himself. "I've never seen anyone pull out a protractor to figure out the best way to fit their sofa through the front door. Nobody pauses mid-dinner to calculate the circumference of their pizza before taking a bite. Real life seems more about winging it—eyeballing measurements, estimating times, and hoping for the best."

When adults openly confess their maths struggles, it sends a sneaky little message: it's okay to hate maths. It's like a secret permission slip to give up. 'If they couldn't master it,' you think, 'why should I bother? They're successful and didn't need to know the square root of 64. So why should I care about finding the area of a triangle?' Suddenly, the struggle feels pointless, like trying to teach a cat to swim.

These are just a few of the reasons why maths is not hot for Jahman. This is why he says to himself nearly every day, 'Maths is not hot.' But are these the only reasons why Jahman constantly drifts off into a daydream during maths lessons?

Why can't he focus? Why does his mind keep wandering, and—let's be honest—why is he always thinking about jollof rice with jerk chicken, even when the teacher's explaining

Pythagoras' Theorem? It's like he's stuck in some kind of food trance, imagining that perfect plate of jollof rice while the numbers on the board just blur into oblivion. Seriously, what's the deal? Why does maths feel like such a drag for Jahman when a delicious plate of jollof is the only thing that seems to get his attention? Why does he find maths more complicated than trying to figure out which seasoning makes jerk chicken just right?

Is it because maths is just *not* his taste, like how some people can't stand pineapple on pizza? Or is it something deeper? Maybe it's the way maths is presented to him. Could the way it's taught just doesn't speak to Jahman? After all, if someone handed him a recipe for jerk chicken, he'd be all over it—but equations? Nah, that's a whole different story. Could it be the curriculum that's just too...boring? Or maybe the teachers aren't bringing the fun? After all, when you're learning about multiplying fractions, it's hard to

Maths Is Not Hot

get excited about it when all you really want is to multiply your servings of jollof rice.

Or is it something intrinsic about maths that makes Jahman feel switched off? Does he get lost in the numbers and formulas the same way someone gets lost in the kitchen, trying to figure out the perfect ratio of spice to heat in a dish? What is stopping Jahman from clicking with maths the way he clicks with food? Is it just a clash of interests, or is it something about how maths just *isn't* the fun, flavourful, fulfilling experience he's looking for?

Whatever it is, Jahman's got questions, and he's pretty sure the answer isn't found in an algebraic expression. So, what's really going on with him and maths? What's the root of the problem? The next chapter is about to dive deep and explain it all, and trust me—it will be a lot more flavourful than a math lesson!

Chapter 6: Why Maths Lessons Miss the Mark for Jahman

Do I enjoy the way maths is taught at school? Absolutely not. In fact, if maths were a person, Jahman and I would block its number and avoid eye contact in the hallway. And no, it's not because I've got some irrational fear of numbers (although, to be fair, they do sometimes feel like the villains in a horror movie). The real issue? The way it's taught makes me want to run screaming in the opposite direction.

The problem

Here's the problem: maths lessons are obsessed with procedural knowledge—memorising steps to solve problems—without ever diving into the good stuff: conceptual knowledge. You know, the 'why' and 'how' behind what we're doing. Instead, every class feels like a never-ending episode of *Maths Robots*, where I'm programmed to follow a series of instructions:

Step 1: Do this.

Step 2: Do that.

Step 3: Voilà, there's your answer!

Cool, I guess? Except I'm left staring at the board thinking, 'Okay, but WHY are we doing this? And what does it even mean?'

Maths class is like being handed a recipe with zero context. Sure, I can follow the steps to bake a cake, but what's the point if no one tells me what flavour it's supposed to be? Am I making chocolate, vanilla, or some weird experimental carrot-banana hybrid? What if nobody I know even likes cake? Without knowing the bigger picture, it all feels pointless.

Here's how it goes: the teacher says, "To find x, you do A, then B, and bam—there's x!" And

I'm like, "Great, but why do I care about x? What did x ever do for me?" It's like trying to build a house without understanding what a blueprint is. Sure, I might stack some bricks, but the result is going to look more like modern art than a liveable home.

It's all about context

At the end of the day, I just want to know why I'm doing what I'm doing. I don't need to be a robot—just give me some context, show me how this fits into the real world, and then maybe, just maybe, I'll start caring about all those x's and y's. But until then, Maths? You're just not my vibe.

Maths and I have never been BFFs (best friends forever) because it's like floating in some abstract, number-filled void where nothing connects to real life. I, just like Jahman, even tried asking my teachers, "Why are we doing this?" And you know what I get? Vague answers or the dreaded, "You'll need this someday." Really?

When was anyone last to find x in the cereal aisle? Until someone explains how this stuff matters, it feels like solving puzzles nobody asked for.

And don't get me started on the lack of real-life applications. When has a teacher ever said, "Here's how you'll use this in your future job or daily life"? Instead, we're stuck solving ancient riddles about trains traveling in opposite directions. (Pro tip: I don't even take the train.)

What I care about is figuring out practical stuff—like calculating interest on a bank loan, budgeting for my dream sneakers, or making the perfect Sunday pancakes without running out of ingredients. But instead of learning how to manage my money or plan for the future, I'm forever finding the area of triangles for reasons that remain a mystery.

Sure, knowing how to calculate a triangle's area might be useful if I'm ever building a treehouse or constructing a pyramid (because that's totally on my to-do list), but until then? No thanks. Meanwhile, I'm out here trying to figure out how many hours I need to work to afford takeout and still save for a concert ticket. You know, real maths.

If maths lessons connected to the real world, I might actually start to care. Show me how to use percentages to snag a discount on those limited-edition Jordans or how to calculate fuel efficiency for my future car. Teach me how to manage a budget so I can survive growing up without having to Google 'how to avoid being broke' every other week.

But instead, maths feels stuck in its little bubble of equations and formulas that have no bearing on what I care about. It's as if maths is a magician pulling rabbits out of a hat but refusing to show me how the trick works. Where's the practical magic?

So, is it any surprise Jahman's not bouncing into class shouting, "Yay, it's maths time!"? Of course not. Instead, he's slouched at his desk, counting down the minutes, and hoping the bell saves him from another round of Mystery Numbers: The Sequel. Until maths becomes less about following steps and more about understanding life, don't expect me—or Jahman— to change my mind. Maths, as it stands? Still not hot.

Let me set the scene for you, Mr OFSTED. Imagine this: Jahman is sitting in maths class, trying to wrap his head around faces, vertices, edges, volume, surface area, and nets of 3D shapes. Sounds straightforward, right? Except there's one tiny problem—there isn't a single actual 3D shape in sight. Not one. Nada. The teacher is passionately describing cubes, pyramids, and spheres like they're mythical creatures, and Jahman's stuck squinting at a flat drawing on the board, trying to imagine what these shapes actually look like in the real world.

It's like being asked to learn how to swim without ever stepping into water. How is anyone supposed to understand the volume of a cube if they can't even see or touch one? If you're going to talk about pyramids, at least bring in a model—or better yet, let students hold it in their hands, spin it around, and actually interact with it. Maths is supposed to be practical, isn't it? Then why does it feel like I'm solving a riddle with half the clues missing?

But wait, Mr Education Secretary, I'm just getting warmed up.

And it's all about monologues

Here's another reason maths just doesn't spark joy for me. Picture this: Jahman walks into class, ready to tackle a new topic, only for the teacher to launch into a never-ending monologue. From the moment the lesson starts to the final bell, it's just them, talking. And talking. And talking. It's like being stuck in a maths-themed podcast that nobody asked for.

Does this make any sense to you? Maths isn't meant to be a one-way street. It's not something you can just absorb passively, like listening to a bedtime story (and trust me, these lectures are more likely to put kids to sleep than inspire a love for algebra). At least give them a chance to chime in! Ask them a question, even if it's just to see if they have any clue what's going on. Or better yet, let them work in groups to crack a problem together.

Collaboration is the secret sauce of learning, but maths teachers act like it's some kind of forbidden fruit. Why? They just keep droning on, as if the only way to learn is by being a human sponge, soaking up endless streams of words and equations. Spoiler alert: it's not.

Teamwork

And now for the pièce de résistance—let's talk about teamwork. You know Usain Bolt, right? The fastest man alive, with a jaw-dropping 100-metre world record of 9.58 seconds. Impressive. But here's a fun fact: when Bolt was part of his relay team, he ran his segment in 9.21 seconds—faster than his solo record. Why? Because of teamwork. The team's seamless baton passes and shared effort pushed him to achieve more than he could alone.

Now, imagine if maths lessons embraced that same spirit of collaboration. Instead of struggling alone, we could team up, brainstorm ideas, share strategies, and tackle problems together. Maths could go from being a lonely grind to an exhilarating team sport.

But first, we need to ditch the never-ending lectures. Give us the tools to succeed—hands-on models, real-world problems, and the power of collaboration. If Usain Bolt needed a team to break records, why should we be expected to conquer the world of maths on our own?

Maths doesn't have to be this endless uphill battle. It could be dynamic, interactive, and dare I say it—fun. But until that happens? Maths is still not hot.

Challenges

Here's why maths sometimes feels like it's stuck in neutral for me or Jahman: it's just not challenging enough! I'm talking about the same rinse-and-repeat basics every single day. Once I've zipped through my work, I'm left staring at the clock, trapped in a time warp where every second feels like an eternity. And if I dare whisper to a friend to save myself from total brain rot? Cue the teacher's death glare, like I've just hacked into the school's wi-fi to stream cat videos during class. But honestly—can you blame me?

Maths Is Not Hot

Let me ask this: why can't maths lessons have a bit more flair, a touch of pizzazz? Where's the thrill of a real brain-bender? Doesn't my teacher realise there's magic in a problem so tricky it makes you question your life choices—until that glorious lightbulb moment hits? Solving a tough maths problem is like beating the final boss in a video game or finding out the plot twist in a mystery novel. It's exhilarating, satisfying, and makes you feel like you've unlocked a new level of genius. Who wouldn't want that?

Take the UKMT Maths Challenge, for example. Every year, they roll out these devilishly clever questions that demand creativity and out-of-the-box thinking. They're hard, no doubt, but they're also ridiculously fun—and there's actual glory at the end! Shiny certificates, a boost to your ego, and bragging rights? Yes, please! Why not use that kind of challenge as inspiration in classes?

Imagine a lesson where instead of just grinding through another worksheet, we're handed puzzles that stretch our brains to the limit. Give me a problem so tricky I have to team up with friends, draw diagrams, and maybe even break into a sweat. Let me wrestle with it, fail, try again, and then have that epic 'aha!' moment. That kind of maths would make me look forward to class, not just survive it.

Maths doesn't have to be a never-ending loop of routine drills—it could be a thrilling adventure. Let's make it happen!

Technology—or lack of it

Let's talk about the elephant in the classroom: technology. We're living in a world of gadgets, apps, and memes, yet maths lessons are stuck in the chalk-and-duster Stone Age. Why? We spend hours at home gaming, solving puzzles, or watching YouTube tutorials on how to fold a fitted sheet. So why not harness that same tech-savvy energy for maths?

Imagine this: instead of trudging through worksheets, we're diving into interactive apps, online simulations, or gamified learning platforms. Picture an algebra game where solving equations unlocks new levels, earns you points, or lets you customise your avatar. Or an app that brings 3D shapes to life—no more guessing what a dodecahedron looks like when you can spin it around on your tablet like a virtual fidget spinner. Maths could be fun. Yes, I said it. Fun.

And let's not stop there. Can we talk about the magic of apps like Desmos or GeoGebra? Drawing graphs by hand is all well and good, but watching a parabola spring to life on a screen? That's like going from a stick figure to a Pixar animation in seconds. Suddenly, equations stop being these abstract riddles and become living, breathing concepts. It's mesmerising—and way more exciting than copying notes off a whiteboard.

Now, let me add my tuppence here, Jahman-style: imagine a maths lesson where you're not just passively listening but actively exploring, experimenting, and discovering. You're using tech to visualise problems, solve challenges, and feel that glorious rush of achievement when it all clicks. It's like being a scientist in a digital lab, except that instead of creating Frankenstein's monster, you're mastering quadratic equations.

So, for the love of all that's logical, make maths modern! Give us the tools, the apps, and the freedom to make it our own. Maths doesn't have to be this dry, one-dimensional slog we endure just to tick a box. It can be dynamic, interactive, and yes, even cool. Who knows? The right tech might even keep me from chatting in class. (Okay, let's not get carried away—but close.)

Just cramming

Here's another one for you, Mr. Education Minister: maths lessons feel like we're stuck in some kind of endless hamster wheel. Every single class is a frantic sprint—rushing through formulas, cramming for tests, and trying to remember just enough to survive the next exam. And then what? The moment the test is over, poof! All those carefully memorised formulas vanish faster than a Snapchat streak. It's not learning; it's maths boot camp.

Right now, maths lessons are like a poorly aimed dodgeball—hurled at us with maximum speed and minimal accuracy. One minute, we're wobbling through fractions; the next, we're drowning in algebra, gasping for air. There's no time to stop, no time to breathe, and certainly no time to ask, "Wait, why are we doing this?" It's chaotic, frustrating, and leaves us with more questions than answers. If maths were a video game, we'd all be stuck on Level 1, mashing buttons and hoping for the best.

But maths doesn't have to feel like an Olympic event. Imagine if we slowed down for a second. What if we had the time to actually process what we're learning, instead of just scrambling to keep up? Picture a lesson where you're not just treading water but diving deep— exploring concepts, solving puzzles, and building real confidence. Maths could actually feel like a subject we can master, instead of a relentless treadmill that's always one step ahead of us.

Frantic teaching; frantic learning

And don't even get me started on the high-speed-chase approach to teaching. It's as if the syllabus is a sacred scroll that cannot be delayed, no matter what. Teachers zip through topics like they're training students for the Maths Grand Prix. Fractions? Done. Angles? Check. Polygons? Blink, and you'll miss them. By the time you've figured out the difference between a scalene and isosceles triangle, the lesson has sped off into cumulative frequency territory. It's exhausting!

Learning maths like this is like trying to swim in a river that's moving way too fast. You're barely keeping your head above water when the current sweeps you away to the next topic. It's no wonder we feel like we're drowning half the time. How are we supposed to build real skills or confidence when trying to stay afloat?

Let me add another Jahman-style tuppence here: Imagine trying to learn to ride a bike while someone's shouting, "Pedal faster!" but never teaching you how to balance. That's a maths class in a nutshell. We're told to keep moving and keep up, but we're not given the time to understand the *why* behind it all. No wonder maths feels like an endless treadmill instead of something we can actually enjoy.

Mathematics Educational Visits

Mr. Secretary of Education, when was the last time the mathematics department took Jahman and his friends on an eye-popping, brain-tingling, Instagram-worthy educational trip? Exactly. Never.

Meanwhile, Geography has been rolling out the red carpet for Jahman—whisking him off to France to admire the Eiffel Tower, dragging him up Mount Everest (metaphorically, because let's be real, Jahman is not about that hiking life), and letting him bask in the beauty of the natural world.

And History? Oh, History is treating Jahman like royalty—rolling out the red carpet as it whisks him off to the UK Parliament, The Hague, Auschwitz, and every grand hall where people in wigs passionately argued about the fate of empires.

And don't even get me started on the Sciences—they're sauntering into the Science Museum like they invented the periodic table, acting like Nobel Prize winners on a school trip. And Maths? Where has Maths taken Jahman? Nowhere. Just stuck in a classroom, drowning in quadratic equations, sketching velocity-time graphs like it's an Olympic sport, and battling the crushing weight of theorems. No flights. No sightseeing. Just numbers, letters, and pure suffering.

So, Mr. Secretary, you see why Maths is flopping in the fun department? Maybe, just maybe, it's time to give Jahman and his fellow number-crunchers a mathematical adventure worth remembering.

The solution

So here's the dream: slow down. Let us catch our breath! Give us a chance to really soak in what we're learning before we're off to the next thing. Wet our appetite with puzzles, challenges, and maybe even sprinkle in a little tech magic. Show us that maths isn't just something we survive—

it's something we can actually *thrive* in. Teach us how to balance before we start pedalling, and who knows? Maybe we'll even stop staring at the clock. (Alright, maybe not *entirely*—but it's progress.) Maths doesn't have to be a battlefield. It could be an epic adventure! Let's rescue Jahman and his fellow number-crunchers from the eternal torture of Thales' circle theorems and take them somewhere epic:

Bletchley Park – The home of the legendary WWII codebreakers, including Alan Turing. Jahman could see the Enigma Machine in action and uncover the mathematical magic behind cryptography. Who knew maths could be this cool?

The Royal Observatory, Greenwich – Let Jahman stand on the Prime Meridian and witness how mathematics literally defines **time itself.** Plus, he can learn how navigation, longitude, and celestial mechanics all rely on maths (no, not just guessing where north is).

The Museum of the History of Science, Oxford – A treasure trove of mathematical instruments, early calculators, and measuring devices. Jahman can see how maths shaped the world before calculators stole all the glory.

These are just a few of the amazing places that could show Jahman how maths isn't just about textbook suffering—it's everywhere, shaping the world in ways he never imagined.

So, dear Maths Department, set Jahman free! Let him experience maths beyond the whiteboard. Who knows? He might even start enjoying it.

So, let's turn it into one.

So what does Jahman want? Well, he wants to learn from the best in the world. And the next chapter spills the beans on how Jahman and his friends think maths should be taught—by borrowing the coolest tricks from the top educators around the globe. Let's dive in. It's gonna be superb. It's gonna be exciting!

Chapter 7: Learning from the Best Around the World

One dreary Monday afternoon, Jahman found himself scrolling through *The Times* (because even TikTok needs a break sometimes), and he stumbled upon an article about the latest OECD PISA mathematics rankings. "What's this OECD thingy?" he muttered, intrigued. Out of sheer curiosity—and definitely not to avoid his maths homework—he decided to investigate.

It turns out that the OECD (Organisation for Economic Co-operation and Development) runs a big-deal study called the **PISA** (Programme for International Student Assessment). It's basically like the Olympics for fifteen-year-olds' academic skills in reading, science, and, of course, maths. Jahman was hooked.

Maths Is Not Hot

In the 2018 rankings, China stole the spotlight with the gold medal, Singapore followed with silver, and Macao clinched bronze. Meanwhile, the UK? We limped in at 17th place, politely applauding from the sidelines. And the US? Well, they were way back in 37th, somewhere between 'we tried' and 'better luck next time.'

Fast forward to 2022, and the Asian maths titans were still crushing it: Singapore soared to first place, Macao hung onto second, and Taipei proudly claimed third. Even Hong Kong joined the podium party in fourth. The UK had climbed to 11th (yay, progress!), but countries like Estonia (7th) and Switzerland (8th) were still showing us how it's done.

Jahman stared at the numbers, scratching his head, thinking, 'Wait, so if these countries are crushing it, what's their secret sauce? Do they have a magic maths wand or something?' As it turns out, no wands were involved—just a wildly different approach to teaching and learning.

The East Asia Maths Masterclass

Jahman had stumbled upon a revelation that flipped his view of maths on its head. These East Asian countries weren't treating maths like a speed-eating contest. No, they'd elevated it to an art form—focused, collaborative, and grounded in the real world. Who knew maths could actually be… cool?

Here's what made them the Beyoncé of the maths world:

1. Depth Over Breadth

East Asian classrooms focus on depth, not speed. Students master foundational concepts before moving on. (PISA, OECD, 2018).

While Jahman's class felt like binge-watching a series at 2x speed—blowing through topics faster than he could say 'quadratic'—students in places like China and Singapore were simmering in their lessons, soaking up every detail until it all clicked.

2. Teamwork Makes the Dream Work

Students in East Asia thrive on collaboration, using group discussions to deepen understanding and sharpen problem-solving skills. (Professor Andreas Schleicher, OECD, 2019)

Picture maths class as a team sport—no slackers allowed. Brainstorming solutions together, tackling problems as a squad? Jahman could totally vibe with that. 'Maths as a group chat? Count me in!' he thought.

3. Mastery Over Memorisation

Singapore's maths curriculum prioritises mastery. Using concrete, pictorial, and abstract methods ensures real understanding. (Dr. Yeap Ban Har, Singapore Maths Specialist).

Forget just memorising formulas and hoping for the best. In Singapore, students were breaking out visual aids, building models, and connecting the dots in ways that made quadratic equations feel less like alien hieroglyphs and more like a puzzle worth solving.

4. Maths IRL (In Real Life)

In Hong Kong and Shanghai, maths lessons focus on real-world applications, making the subject practical and relevant. (OECD *Insights*, 2019).

While Jahman was still asking, "When will I ever use this?" kids in Hong Kong were budgeting for shopping trips, planning architectural designs, and basically proving maths was their real-life superpower. Suddenly, finding the area of a trapezium didn't seem so pointless.

Jahman couldn't help but compare. His lessons felt like sprinting through a maze blindfolded, while their approach was like solving a Rubik's Cube with a cheat sheet. "What if we slowed down?" he wondered. "What if maths wasn't about racing through the curriculum but actually making sense of it?"

He imagined a UK classroom where lessons weren't just about memorising formulas but applying them. Calculating the best sale at JD Sports? Figuring out the perfect free-kick angle? "Now that's the kind of maths I'd actually use," he said, grinning.

"Why can't maths feel more like a TikTok dance?" Jahman mused. "Fun, purposeful, and something you'd actually want to master?" The answer was obvious: actually, it *could*.

Across the globe, students in East Asia weren't just crushing PISA rankings—they were redefining what it meant to learn maths. They weren't aiming to be the fastest; they were aiming to be the smartest. And that's a vibe Jahman could get behind.

As he closed the article, Jahman felt a spark of hope. Maybe the UK wasn't doomed to be stuck in the middle forever. Maybe, just maybe, we could learn from the best and start turning our maths classrooms into places of creativity, collaboration, and actual fun.

"Watch out, Singapore," he said with a smirk. "The UK is coming for your crown. Eventually." He certainly hoped so. And then he thought, 'Maths might just be the maestro of education— conducting the whole symphony behind the scenes.'

Learning from the Best: Europe's Maths Magic

But wait—it's not just East Asia leading the pack. Closer to home, European countries such as Estonia, Switzerland, the Netherlands, and Finland are also leaving us in the dust. These countries are practically our neighbours, so why aren't we taking a page from their book?

Jahman leans back in his chair, tapping his pencil against the desk. "Wait, Finland?" he said. "Estonia? They're not even that far away. Why are they so ahead of us?" He's always wondered why the UK seems to be stuck in a rut when it comes to maths education. "It's not like they're using some magic formula or something. They've just figured it out. What, do they feed their kids algebra for breakfast?"

In Finland

Here's a fun fact that might blow your mind (and probably leave some teachers clutching their coffee mugs): in Finland, they don't split students into ability groups. That's right—no 'top set' for the brainiacs and no 'bottom set' for the ones who need a little extra help. Every class is a mixed bag, and here's the kicker—it actually works.

According to Sahlberg (2011), Finnish schools rarely divide students by ability, and formal exams don't rear their heads until the very end of secondary school. The focus? Inclusivity and giving every student an equal shot at success.

Jahman's eyebrows shot up so high they nearly left his face. "Wait, no sets? So, is there no maths wizard group and no better luck next time group? How does that even work?" He was flabbergasted. The idea of a classroom without labels was as mind-bending to him as trying to do trigonometry without a calculator.

In the UK, and especially at his school, we're borderline obsessed with ability groupings. Students are sorted into tidy little boxes like 'high flyers' or 'strugglers,' as if we're assembling a pack of assorted biscuits. For those in the lower sets, it's like being handed a flashing neon sign that screams, 'Caution: Not a Maths Person—Handle with Care!'

As education expert Jo Boaler (2015) pointed out, slapping a 'low ability' label on students doesn't just dent their self-esteem—it can lower expectations and drain their motivation faster than a leaking phone battery. Even worse, it often becomes a self-fulfilling prophecy: believe you're terrible at maths, and guess what? You might just prove yourself right.

'Imagine,' Jahman thought, 'a classroom where no one's branded a lost cause or a child prodigy. Just students, learning together, without the pressure to fit into some arbitrary box.' Sounds pretty revolutionary, doesn't it? Or at the very least, like the start of a maths movie where everyone wins.

In Estonia

Fresh from having his mind blown by Finland's 'no-exams, everyone's-a-genius' education vibes, Jahman was practically buzzing to see what Estonia had up its sleeve. Could it really outdo Finland? Did Estonia have some secret maths sauce that made Pythagoras look like a beginner? Jahman was on the edge of his seat, ready to soak up whatever magical, maths-powered wisdom Estonia was about to drop.

Estonia's maths education is like a hidden treasure chest—low-key, brilliant, and totally worth stealing some ideas from! Unlike the test-heavy grind Jahman's used to, Estonia takes a chill but thoughtful approach to learning. No pressure cookers here! As Sahlberg (2016) highlights, kids in Estonia don't have to cram their brains with facts or speed through topics to check off boxes. Instead, the focus is on *why* maths works and solving problems in creative, practical ways.

Jahman's jaw practically hits the desk. "Wait, you're telling me no cramming? No soul-crushing end-of-term exams? Do they actually teach you to understand maths instead of just surviving it? This is wild!"

He leans back, imagining what it would be like to study in a place where maths isn't a monster but a puzzle waiting to be solved. "No stress, just learning? What kind of sweet maths sorcery is this? Estonia, I see you! That's the kind of maths I could actually vibe with."

Turns out, Estonia isn't just about numbers—it's about nurturing curiosity and making maths feel like an adventure, not a chore. And Jahman? He's definitely taking notes.

Estonia isn't just nailing maths—it's practically the tech wizard of the classroom! As one of the most digitally advanced countries on the planet, their schools are decked out with tech so cutting-edge it might as well be straight out of a sci-fi movie (thanks, OECD, 2020). But this isn't just about flashy gadgets; the Estonian Ministry of Education and Culture (2020) says technology is woven into the learning process like chocolate chips in a cookie—essential and irresistible.

Jahman's eyes nearly popped out of his head, and his jaw practically hit the desk. "Wait—so they're using tech to draw those evil cubic and tangent graphs? Meanwhile, I'm over here, waging war with x on a crumpled worksheet like some knight in a medieval maths battle. Where do I sign up? Forget the UK. I'm learning maths in Estonian now. Hey, Mr Richard Branson, my role model—can you fly me to Estonia, please? They've got maths down to an art form. Forget space travel. Let's go straight to maths heaven!"

For the first time, Jahman started to see maths as more than just numbers on a page. Estonia wasn't treating maths like some abstract torture device—it was practical, exciting, and (brace yourself) fun. "Real-world maths that's actually useful?" Jahman grinned. "Now that's the kind of lesson I'd actually look forward to. "Estonia, take a bow. You're officially the MVP of making maths cool, and Jahman is all in."

Changing the focus

Leaning back in his chair, Jahman tapped his fingers on the desk, deep in thought. "Why are we still clinging to outdated methods that divide and discourage?" he muttered, side-eyeing the classroom around him. "If we really want students to excel," he said to no one in particular, "we've got to rethink this whole approach to maths education."

He pauses, a slight grin forming on his face as he thinks about how the countries doing well in maths focus on understanding and mastery rather than rushing through the syllabus. "We should shift the focus to understanding, not just memorising," he says aloud, surprising a couple of classmates nearby. "We need to lift every student, no matter where they start." Jahman's mind races—what if every kid in the class had the time and support to grasp the concepts truly? What if everyone could get the chance to shine? The blueprint for success is right there," Jahman says with newfound determination. "We just need to look around, learn from the best, and build a system where all of us can shine. Imagine what that could look like!" He looks out the window, picturing a classroom where students aren't labelled, where they work together and learn at their own pace. 'That's the dream, right?' he thinks. 'A place where we're all in this together, not racing against each other.'

Jahman sat there, staring at the chalkboard, his mind wandering to a far-off land of jollof rice and jerk chicken, as usual. But then, a thought hit him like a bolt of lightning. "Wait a minute," he muttered to himself. "If the government doesn't want to take a leaf out of the East Asia education playbook, then maybe I should just... run away from maths altogether!"

Escape Plan

He looked around the classroom, trying to imagine a world without algebraic equations, quadratic formulas, and those never-ending word problems. A world where he could exist without the looming threat of a test on Pythagoras' theorem. The more he thought about it, the more his imagination took over. He could feel the escape calling his name—like a pirate, setting sail to a land of no numbers.

'That's it!' Jahman thought. 'I'm done. If the government can't learn from the East, I'll learn from myself. I'll go on a quest for the perfect maths-less subject. A subject that doesn't make me break into a cold sweat every time I hear the word 'trigonometry'.'

And so began Jahman's comedic journey to find the ultimate escape from the world of numbers. He considered all his options—art, music, drama, geography and science... But the road to a maths-free life wasn't going to be easy. He'd have to dodge fractions, sidestep statistics, and outwit the evil forces of geometry.

As he set out on this quest, Jahman realised one thing: the world might be filled with maths, but there was no reason he couldn't have a little fun escaping it. His journey had only just begun, and the road to a maths-free existence promised plenty of laughs, a few bumps, and a whole lot of imagination.

Stay tuned for Jahman's next adventure in seeking for a subject that doesn't require any real numbers.

Chapter 8:
The Journey to Find a Maths-less Subject

Jahman slouched at the corner of the classroom, as usual, staring out the window in search of a squirrel to pass by. "Come on, just one squirrel," he muttered under his breath. He could already feel the panic rising as the teacher's voice blended into the background. *Maths, maths, maths... it's everywhere.*

He sighed deeply, his mind racing. 'I'm from a third-class family, and honestly, when it comes to maths, we're as poor as a mouse in a church. No money, no skills, no hope.' His eyes wandered over to the board where numbers danced like the villains of his nightmares. 'I have dyscalculia, maths anxiety, ADHD... you name it. The government's refusing to abolish maths from my education, even though it's clearly causing me more trauma than a soap opera marathon.'

Jahman leaned back in his chair, propping his feet up on the desk as he stared at the ceiling. "I have no clue when it comes to maths," he said to himself. "It's like trying to read a foreign language... written in invisible ink... while riding a rollercoaster. Why don't I just go find a subject that doesn't involve numbers? Something peaceful, something that won't make my brain feel like it's doing squats without my permission."

As he glanced at the clock, his mind started wandering. 'What if there's a maths-less subject out there just waiting for me? Something where I can finally breathe, where I'm not looking over my shoulder for the next equation to attack me like a rogue ninja.' His thoughts were racing now, visions of a world without maths filling his head.

It's time for the great Jahman's quest for a maths-free subject. "Where to begin?" he mutters to himself. He imagines it: a world where he can be free from the terror of circle theorems. A world where history, drama, and art, to name but a few, take over, where numbers are mere figments of the past. No more trying to figure out why x equals y or why a circle is not a sphere.

The options

His first stop? History class. He imagines himself living in ancient Egypt, chilling with the pharaohs, building pyramids with nothing but bricks, no calculations required. But then his mind starts to wander again. 'Wait, did they have jollof rice in ancient Egypt? Probably not. But hey, I bet they had some spicy food...' He's off again, mentally skipping through time and space, but this time, it's not with a calculator in hand.

Then he thinks about drama. The bright lights of the stage, the magic of performance. He could be the next Shakespeare... or at least the next star of the school play. Acting is easy, right? No numbers to memorise, just lines, gestures, and some occasional exaggerated emotion. *Drama it is.* He's pretty sure he can survive this one unless they ask him to calculate the stage dimensions or time the act with a stopwatch, and then he's done.

But there's another possibility—English. Writing, reading, and exploring different worlds through stories. *No maths.* He could dive into the works of Charles Dickens or start crafting his own novel about the mystical adventures of Jahman, the boy who defeated maths with sheer willpower and a few well-placed jollof rice jokes.

But wait, he thinks, what if the English teacher starts going on about metaphors or similes, or worse—poetry? Can't risk it. He needs a *safe* zone.

Jahman smiles as he remembers one subject he knows won't let him down: physical education. No numbers in PE. Just running, jumping, maybe a bit of football. There, he can shine without worrying about any sort of rearranging of formulas. If anything, he can always get a good workout while dodging maths books on the field. Ah, PE... the haven for people like him who are just trying to survive.

As the bell rings for the end of class, Jahman grabs his bag with a renewed sense of purpose. "That's it," he mutters. "The search for the maths-free subject is on. No more of this number nonsense. It's time to escape and explore the world of things that don't involve algebraic expressions. Who's with me?"

And with that, Jahman walks out of the classroom, already dreaming of the possibilities. There are so many: art, business studies, music... He might not be the next Einstein, but one thing's for sure—he's going to make it through school without letting a single number trip him up. Or at least, that's the plan.

Art

Jahman's journey to escape the clutches of Mr. Maths and his relentless numbers began.

After all, Jahman thought "Man shall not live by maths alone". Maths is not hot.

Jahman started his escape by dashing towards Aunty Art, who was deep in conversation with the legendary Leonardo Da Vinci. "Please, Aunty Art, take me in! Maths and numbers are hot on my trail, and I need refuge!" Jahman begged. "I've heard you help students draw, just draw—nothing else. No maths, no numbers."

Aunty Art smiled. Jahman thought, finally, a subject where numbers won't chase me like a cat after a mouse! He grabbed his sketchpad, ready to unleash his inner Picasso, only for Aunty Art to announce, "Today, we'll be exploring symmetry and the golden ratio." The what?! Before Jahman could even Google 'golden ratio' he was handed a ruler and a protractor. A protractor, in Art! Madam, I came here to draw flowers, not dissect them with geometry. Jahman could swear he heard Pythagoras chuckling from his grave. 'Maths is just everywhere,' thinks Jahman.

'Hold your horses,' Jahman thought. 'Measure what? I came to Aunty Art to escape the horrors of numbers, and now she's telling me to use a ruler. This sounds way too much like Mr Maths' territory!' He put up his hand. "Hold up, Aunty Art," he said, "I thought you were about drawing! Measuring and golden ratio? That's Mr Maths' job, not yours!"

Little did Jahman know that art requires more than just drawing—it demands spatial reasoning, patterns, symmetry, and sometimes even the golden ratio! It turns out that the genius Leonardo Da Vinci allegedly used the golden ratio to design his masterpiece, the Mona Lisa.

Jahman paused and thought to himself, 'What a wonderful world…' and then he realised this was all connected to maths.

Business Studies

After Aunty Art's unfortunate betrayal, Jahman was determined to find refuge elsewhere. As he wandered, deep in thought, he spotted Mr Moneyman, Business Studies, dashing towards NatWest Bank with a stack of papers tucked under his arm. His polished shoes gleamed under the sunlight, and his confident stride screamed 'CEO in the making'. Jahman perked up immediately.

"Hello, Mr Business Studies! I love business studies!" Jahman called out, panting as he chased after him. "I have so many business ideas. Will you give me the chance to join your class? I want to become a millionaire, maybe even a billionaire, or at least rich enough to buy a meal deal without checking my bank balance first!"

Mr Business Studies stopped in his tracks, turned to face Jahman, and flashed a welcoming smile. "You're welcome! Grab your book, let's get started," he said with the enthusiasm of someone who truly believed in turning dreams into profit. "Here's a question for you," he added, pulling out a crisp sheet of paper.

He began, "A machine costs £10,000. It depreciates by 20% each year. How much will it be worth after three years?"

Jahman froze, his jaw practically hitting the pavement. His mind screamed in protest. "Mr. Business, this is just a repeated percentage by Mr. Maths!" he retorted, throwing his hands in the air as if he were filing a complaint. "I thought we were here to discuss business ideas like starting a smoothie empire or building the next Tesla!"

Mr Business Studies chuckled, his laugh as polished as his shoes. "This is called the reducing balance method in Business Studies," he explained patiently, as though that made it any better.

Jahman paused, narrowing his eyes at him. "Why didn't you tell me you have a joint account with Mr. Maths?" he asked, his tone dripping with mock betrayal. "You've been working with him all along, haven't you? First percentages, now depreciation? What next—compound interest?"

Mr. Business Studies laughed even harder this time, patting Jahman on the shoulder like a mentor soothing a frustrated apprentice. "Without Mr. Maths, I couldn't function. How else would I calculate profits, costs or even investments?" he replied with a wink that was supposed to comfort Jahman.

Jahman's heart sank. Once again, Mr. Maths had managed to infiltrate another subject. He stared blankly at Mr. Business Studies as he walked away, probably heading to finalise a deal worth millions. Jahman shuffled off in the opposite direction, muttering under his breath, "Maths is not hot. Not even in Business."

Drama

There she was, the beauty queen of Drama, twirling effortlessly across the floor, the sound of Master KG's 'Jerusalema ikhaya lami' filling the *Strictly Come Dancing* studios with its infectious rhythm. Her steps were so graceful she seemed to be floating in the air, her shimmering dress catching the light as if she were the muse of the disco ball. Jahman stood there, mesmerised, until the Drama teacher spotted him lurking at the edge of the stage. She waved him over with a curious smile.

"Hello, kiddie, you look morose. What's the matter?" she asked, tilting her head with theatrical concern.

Jahman let out a dramatic sigh to match the mood. "Hmmm. I've been travelling the world, Drama Queen, trying to find a subject where I can finally be happy. But wherever I go, the devil—Maths and numbers—seems to follow me like a shadow. They've already devoured my entire family, and now they're after me. Could you save me, Drama? You just act and dance, right? No calculators, no equations, just pure emotion?"

She gave Jahman a twinkle-eyed grin; the kind that makes you think you're about to walk straight into trouble. "Alright, everyone!" she suddenly shouted to the room. "Put on your dancing shoes, divide yourselves into groups of four, and set the stage lights to a 45-degree angle!"

Jahman froze in horror, his theatrical dreams shattering into a million algebraic shards. "Wait—what? Angle? Divide?! These are Mr. Maths' cursed words! What are they doing in Drama?" His voice cracked like an untrained actor at their first audition.

He could feel the room spinning as his Maths PTSD kicked in. Groups of four? Jahman couldn't even divide a sandwich evenly in Maths class, let alone people! And a 45-degree angle? He thought that nonsense was reserved for protractors and triangle diagrams, not stage lighting!

Quickly, Jahman started packing his imaginary belongings into an invisible suitcase, mumbling incoherently. 'Let me get out of here before MI6 or NASA comes after me for failing another Maths mission. I couldn't even divide numbers in Maths—how can I divide pupils into groups of 4? Are you *non compos mentis*? I don't want any blood on my hands when I miscalculate and someone ends up in a group of three! That's what this is—utter madness!'

He turned to flee, his feet carrying him out of the Drama studio as fast as a badly choreographed routine. Behind him, he could hear the Drama teacher laughing like the villain in an opera. Maths had infiltrated Drama, and Jahman's dreams of finding a haven were officially dashed. Again.

PE

After fleeing the Drama Queen, Jahman spotted Mr Sporty, PE, energetically coaching a group of athletes while simultaneously working with Lewis Hamilton to keep him in peak shape for the Silverstone Grand Prix. He stood tall, whistle swinging from his neck like a medal, exuding the confidence of someone who'd never had a run-in with the horrors of quadratic equations.

"Hello, Mr Sporty! I'm all yours!" Jahman shouted enthusiastically, jogging over like a kid at recess. "Maths and numbers are chasing me like the police after a terrorist, but I'm not a terrorist— I'm just a poor soul searching for greener pastures! Please, Mr PE, sign me up. I know you just run around like kids do on the playground. No numbers, no problems, right?"

Mr PE gave Jahman a long, knowing look and said, "Alright, let's see how you do. Take the tape and measure 100 metres. Did you know Usain Bolt ran it in 9.58 seconds? That's the World Record. Now, calculate his speed."

Jahman froze mid-step, staring at him as if he'd just asked him to divide by zero. "What? You, Mr PE? Problem-solving in PE? I thought your job was just running, jumping, and blowing that whistle like an over-enthusiastic referee! I remember speed and formulas from Mr Maths, but I didn't sign up for this." Jahman's voice rose dramatically. "Speed equals Distance divided by Time. That's Maths territory! Please, Mr. PE, don't start copying Mr. Maths—it's not healthy! Think of the children!"

But Mr PE was relentless, a statue of discipline, waiting for Jahman to finish the calculation. Jahman panicked, dropping the tape measure and backing away slowly. "You know what, Mr. PE?" Jahman said with a nervous grin. "Catch me if you're Usain Bolt! I'm out of here!"

Jahman turned and sprinted as fast as he could—not 100 metres, but far enough to escape the madness. Behind him, he could hear Mr. PE laughing, the sound of his whistle echoing in the distance. "See you in the next generation!" Jahman called back. Maths—definitely not hot—had once again invaded his safe space.

English

After Miss Borrower, English, had finished struggling to borrow more words from Dutch, German, French, and Greek at the UN conference in Geneva, Jahman tentatively approached her.

"Hello, Miss Parrot English! I love to read, but... I can't read," Jahman lied, trying his best to look pitiful and earnest. "Will you take me on board?"

Miss English smiled knowingly, adjusting her glasses. "No problem, Mr. Renegade. Let's start with phonics. Phonics follows patterns, just like the patterns in Maths."

The moment she mentioned Maths, a chill shot down Jahman's spine. Patterns? In English? His mind screamed for an escape route. He thought to himself, I wish I were an alien right now, hiding on some distant planet where Maths doesn't exist. How has Mr. Maths managed to infiltrate English in all subjects? Is there nowhere safe?

Miss English continued, oblivious to Jahman's internal panic. "For example, 'ai' sounds like the name of the letter A in the alphabet. So we have words like 'aid,' 'paid,' 'rain,' 'train,' and 'drain.' They all share the distinctive 'ai' sound. Do you see the pattern?"

Jahman's head spun as he tried to process this betrayal. English—his safe haven—was using Maths-like patterns to teach phonics? He muttered under his breath, "I don't die. Maths is everywhere. Chineke, take me now!"

But it got worse. Miss English, with a twinkle in her eye, asked Jahman to come up with more words following the 'ai' pattern. He raised his trembling hand hesitantly. "Miss English, I have a question. Why do we pronounce 'said' as (/sɛd/) even though it has 'ai' in it? Shouldn't it be pronounced (/seid/) like 'aid,' 'rain,' or 'train'?"

She gave him a smile that was part sympathy, part amusement, and replied, "Ah, English has exceptions. Patterns only take us so far."

Exceptions?! Jahman's brain was short-circuiting. Not only had Maths wormed its way into English, but now even the patterns weren't reliable. He felt betrayed twice over. Patterns and exceptions, phonics and Maths—it was all too much. He staggered out of the room, mumbling to himself, "There is no escape! Mr. Maths is lurking everywhere!"

Music

After defeating Madam English for the first time (and yes, it felt like a victory in a battle royale), Jahman stumbled upon something that could only be described as destiny. There, in the middle of Roundwood Park, he met the one and only Mr. Music Man, trotting along with Bob Marley's iconic hit 'No Woman, No Cry' blasting from his portable speaker, jumping up and down like a crazy horse on a sugar rush. The rhythm was infectious—Jahman's feet immediately started tapping, and he felt as if he was in the middle of a music video, except he wasn't sure if he was dancing or just trying to avoid tripping on a stray tree root.

He couldn't resist. Jahman approached with all the enthusiasm of someone who had just discovered a hidden treasure chest. "Hello, Mr. Music Man! I really love reggae," he blurted out. "I want to reincarnate as the maestro himself, Bob Marley. Could you take me on as your protégé?

Because, well, Mr. Maths is literally devouring my entire family."

Mr. Music Man stopped mid-jump, looked Jahman square in the eyes, and said, "Ah, my young reggae apprentice, I see you have the spirit of music, but to master it, you must understand the rhythms. Music, like life, is a balance, and so is maths. Now, imagine this: You're composing a new reggae song inspired by the great Bob Marley himself. Your song will have 4 beats in each measure (4/4 time signature, of course), and you want to add a cool rhythm with different note values. Here's the question, mate: If you place one-half note (2 beats), two-quarter notes (1 beat each), and four eighth notes (1/2 beat each) in the second measure, how many total beats will you have in the second measure? Does this combination fit into the 4/4 time signature?"

Jahman blinked. His mind was suddenly hit with the rhythm of maths—fractions, notes, beats.

'Wait, hold up,' he thought to himself. 'Fractions in Mr. Maths? In reggae music? Who on earth is this Mr. Maths to be infiltrating Bob Marley's soul-soothing rhythms? I thought I was here to vibe with music, not do maths!'

But Jahman wasn't about to back down. He shook his head and smiled, thinking, 'Yes, Woman Dey Cry. Fractions from Mr. Maths in music? This is madness!'

He started working through the beats: A half note = 2 beats.

Two-quarter notes = 1 beat each, so that's 2 beats.

Four eighth notes = 1/2 beat each, which adds up to 2 beats.

Total beats in the second measure = 2 + 2 + 2 = 6 beats.

Jahman couldn't help but laugh to himself. "Wait, this is too much! This doesn't fit into 4 beats. It's like trying to squeeze a whole pizza into a lunchbox—it's just not gonna work!"

Feeling frustrated but amused, Jahman turned to Mr. Music Man and said, "I really do love reggae, but man, I didn't sign up for fractions and quarter notes. Can't we just vibe without all the numbers? I'm trying to be a reggae star, not a maths genius!"

Mr. Music Man chuckled, his dreadlocks bouncing with every laugh. "Ah, I see you, my young apprentice. But trust me, understanding the rhythm of music and maths is the same. They both have a flow—just like Bob Marley's timeless beats. But sometimes, you gotta get into the groove of it all. Now, go ahead, solve that riddle of the rhythms, and maybe—just maybe—you'll see how math can help you write the perfect song."

And just like that, with a wink and a nod, he went back to grooving to 'No Woman, No Cry', as if Jahman hadn't just had his brain hijacked by fractions in music. Jahman stood there for a moment, contemplating: Should he really pursue being a reggae star, or should he just go hide from Mr. Maths and his tricky questions?

But as the beat dropped again, Jahman couldn't help but feel that maybe—just maybe—he was one step closer to understanding how everything, even maths, could come together in perfect harmony.

'Alright, Mr. Music,' Jahman thought, 'Maybe we'll give this whole fraction thing one more try... just don't ask me to calculate the number of beats in a reggae solo, or I might have to run for the hills!'

Science: Physics

One serene evening, as Jahman was taking a quiet promenade through the peaceful countryside, trying to shake off the trauma of another Maths-filled day, he happened upon

Madam Science and her three children—Biology, Chemistry, and Physics—standing side by side at an astronomical observatory. They were gazing at the moon and stars, looking like the royal family of the cosmos. Jahman thought, 'Ah, finally, a break from all this numerical chaos. These subjects seem to have escaped the clutches of Mr. Maths and his ruthless algorithms!'

But of course, just as Jahman was about to take in the peace and beauty of the night sky, Madam Science turned to him with a piercing gaze and asked, "My son, why are you sweating like a fish out of water?"

Jahman gasped for air, feeling the heat rise in his cheeks as if he were standing in a furnace. "It's Maths and Numbers, Madam. They've turned my life into a flaming inferno. I can't escape them! They haunt me like a shadow." He wiped the sweat from his forehead dramatically. "Please, Madam Science, can you grant me a moment of peace and let me into your humble abode? I can't take much more of this fire and brimstone that Maths brings!"

Physics, the eldest of Madam Science's children, stepped forward with an air of calm authority. He was holding a piece of chalk, tapping it against the side of his notepad like a professor ready to deliver a life-changing lecture. "Sure, take your book and work this out, then. Calculate the volume of a gold bar with a mass of 250g and a density of $2.6g/cm^3$. Remember to make the volume the subject of the formula."

Jahman froze in place, his heart doing somersaults in his chest. "Change of subject?" he stammered. His brain was short-circuiting again. "I remember that phrase from Mr. Maths and Numbers! What is changing the subject here in Physics? This is an ambush! I thought Physics was about rockets and explosions, not algebra and rearranging equations!" He looked around desperately, half-expecting to see Mr. Maths pop up out of nowhere, grinning like a villain. "I'm flabbergasted!" Jahman cried. "First Drama, now Physics?! What is this—Maths in disguise?"

As Madam Science and her children exchanged knowing glances, Jahman realised the truth: no subject was safe. Mr. Maths had infiltrated everything, turning his once-peaceful world into a chaotic mess of formulas and functions. "Maths is not hot!" Jahman muttered under his breath as he started backing away slowly, like someone trying to escape a wild animal. The cosmos was no longer his safe haven. Maths had followed him here, too.

Science: Chemistry

Feeling utterly betrayed by Physics, Jahman thought, 'Enough! This is it. I'm going to find my safe space in Chemistry, the second-born of Madam Science. Surely, it's all about those vibrant, colourful reactions and things going boom—no Maths allowed, right?' Jahman entered the Chemistry lab with a gleam of hope, imagining bubbling test tubes and harmless experiments. But alas, his dreams were about to be shattered once again.

The first thing Madam Chemistry said, with a twinkle in her eye (that Jahman should have recognised as a warning sign), was, "Alright, let's balance this chemical equation."

Jahman threw his hands up to the heavens. "Lord, have mercy on me!" he cried. "Excuse me?! Balance a chemical equation? I thought I left that nightmare back in Mr. Maths' class, where the equations were as cruel as they were numerous! And as if that wasn't bad enough," Jahman gasped, his voice rising, "she starts talking about molar ratios and Avogadro's number. Who even is Avogadro, and why does he need a number?!" Jahman demanded, looking around the room as if expecting Avogadro himself to materialise and explain this madness. *I came here for explosions, not fractions!* Was this a chemistry class or a twisted Maths seminar disguised as a laboratory experiment? Jahman could feel panic rising in his chest like a bubbling potion gone wrong.

Honestly, suppose the periodic table is a party. In that case, Maths is the uninvited guest who refuses to leave—hovering in the corner, sipping punch, and making awkward small talk about algebra. "Why is he here?!" Jahman muttered, pointing at the smug, square-shaped numbers that appeared on every equation.

Madam Chemistry, utterly oblivious to Jahman's internal breakdown, cheerfully continued, "Now let's calculate the molar mass of sulphuric acid..."

Jahman could barely hear her over the deafening sound of his soul leaving his body. *Maths is* everywhere—everywhere! If Jahman wanted to play with fireworks, why was he doing fraction-based gymnastics? Maths is not hot—it's an unwanted guest at the coolest party, and I've had enough of it. I bet even oxygen molecules are out here secretly solving equations while I'm just trying to breathe in peace.

Science: Biology

Biology, the youngest of Madam Science's trio, tapped Jahman gently on the shoulder with a smile that could only mean trouble. "Welcome to the subject of life, birth, and growth, Mr. Fugitive," she said warmly, as if she was welcoming him into a cozy, safe space. "Here's a question just for you."

Jahman looked at her, a mix of curiosity and terror bubbling up. "Oh no, not again," he muttered under his breath.

She handed him a piece of paper, practically glowing with optimism. "A biologist is studying a colony of bacteria that doubles in size every 3 hours. The initial population is 500 bacteria. How many bacteria will there be after 12 hours?"

Jahman froze, staring at the question as if it was written in a foreign language. "What are you talking about, Madam Birth?" he asked, his voice trembling. "This question screams 'exponential growth'—and that belongs to Mr. Maths!" He waved his hands frantically in the air as if trying to shoo away the invisible force that had attached itself to Biology. "What is it doing here? Why is Mr. Maths tormenting my life at every turn? I can't escape him! First, he was in Physics, then Chemistry, and now... now he's here, hiding in Biology behind bacteria!"

As the room spun around Jahman like a bad acid trip from the depths of a number-filled nightmare, he knew he had reached his limit. The walls were closing in, and the very idea of 'doubling' bacteria every few hours was enough to send his brain into overdrive. "I can't take any more!" he shouted, clutching his head like it was about to explode.

He collapsed to the floor with dramatic flair, his body hitting the ground like a badly choreographed fall in a soap opera. The next thing Jahman knew, he woke up in a hospital bed at St. Mary's, staring up at the sterile white ceiling, his heart racing. His hand instinctively reached for a piece of paper nearby. It was just a note from Biology, taunting him with more numbers. *500 bacteria doubling every 3 hours.* The horror!

Computer Science

Jahman woke up from his slumber, his head feeling as if it had been through a blender, only to find Dr. Computer Science standing next to him, clipboard in hand, looking far too cheerful for someone who was about to ruin his day.

"Hello, Mr. Fugitive," Dr. Computer Science said with a grin that could only mean trouble. "How are we feeling today? Would you like to join my C++ company and learn how to write your own algorithm?"

Jahman blinked a few times, unsure if he was still dreaming. "Algo-wat, Doc?!" he mumbled, trying to make sense of the madness. Algorithms? The only 'algorithm' Jahman knew was algebra from Mr. Maths, and that was the stuff of nightmares. What sort of cheese is an algorithm, and why is it invading his peaceful existence now?

"Maths is not hot," Jahman whispered to himself as his head spun.

"Doc, let's be real here," he said, shaking his head. "I couldn't even handle the one lonely plus sign in Mr. Maths' lessons. Now you're throwing two of them at me with a capital C?! What do you want me to do with that?!"

He paused for dramatic effect, his eyes widening as the realisation hit him. "The last time I saw a 'C' that this important was Einstein's theory of relativity—C as the speed of light. So,

Doc, by the time you beep again, I'll be long gone... at light speed!"

And with that, Jahman stood up in one swift motion, gliding toward the door, but not before turning to give Dr. Computer Science one last look. "See you in the next dimension!" he shouted. With a flourish, he vanished into thin air, leaving Dr. Computer Science standing in stunned silence, staring at an empty hospital bed. Another narrow escape. Maths, once again, had tried to trap Jahman, but he was faster than the speed of light.

Geography

Jahman reappeared on top of Scafell Pike, thinking he had finally escaped everyone—no Maths, no numbers, just fresh air and the sound of the wind in the mountains. 'Freedom at last!' Jahman thought as he gazed out at the breathtaking view. But, of course, it was too good to be true. Out of nowhere, he spotted Madam

Earth herself, aka Miss Geography, strutting across the mountain in a stunning fuchsia pink dress and matching black Valentino Garavani stilettos, her heels clicking on the rocky terrain as if she were walking down a runway.

"Hello, Mr. Maths-Phobia, what brings you here?" Miss Geography asked, twirling like a fashion icon posing for a photo shoot.

Jahman stood motionless, his jaw practically hitting the ground. "Wait, how do you know me?" he stammered, wondering if she had a crystal ball or if she was just stalking him through the wilderness.

Miss Geography raised an eyebrow, her expression unfazed. "Who doesn't know you? Even MI6 has your picture on their most-wanted list," she replied coolly. 'Great,' Jahman thought. As if things weren't bad enough. Now he's public enemy number one for escaping Maths.

"Fair enough," Jahman muttered. "I hear you love travelling a lot, and honestly, I envy your students. Could you take me on board? I'd love to tag along on one of your field trips. Anything to escape Maths for a while."

Miss Geography flashed a smile, one that could probably stop traffic. "You've come to the right place, Mr Prodigal Son," she said with a wink. "Our next field trip is to calculate the population density of Harlesden—that is, the number of people living per square kilometre. Feel free to join us!"

Jahman froze yet again. "Wait a minute, Miss Geography. I know 'density' from Mr. Maths and Mr. Physics, but population density? Is this Archimedes' density or Stephen Hawking's density?!" he spluttered, clutching his head as if he had just been hit by a freight train of confusion.

He paused, trying to catch his breath. "Wow, I never knew density was so marketable! It's everywhere! Density in Maths, density in Physics, and now density in Geography? Is there a density in Catering too? Maybe I missed that in Home Economics. If so, I might just become Superman. But wait, do I get a cape with this density deal?"

Miss Geography smiled sweetly, her stilettos digging into the earth, anchoring the world in place. "Well, Mr. Prodigal Son, I'm afraid there's no cape for you in Geography, but there's plenty more where that came from. You might want to brush up on your spatial awareness next. After all, that's where Maths and Geography collide."

"Maths?" Jahman gasped, horrified. "You're telling me Maths is involved here too? I thought Geography was all about mountains, rivers, and landmarks, not... numbers and calculations!"

Jahman took one last look at the stunning mountain view, now tainted with the dreaded spectre of Maths. "I need a vacation from this entire Maths conspiracy. Next thing I know, I'll be calculating the distance between myself and a landmine of equations!"

History

In Jahman's desperate quest to escape the clutches of Mr. Maths, he stumbled upon Grandpa History—none other than the almighty chronicler of time himself—wandering the hallowed grounds of the Battle of Waterloo. He was stooped over, magnifying glass in hand, examining a cannonball as if he were a detective in a crime drama. Apparently, he was searching for yet another piece of evidence to rewrite the story of that legendary battle.

Seizing the moment, Jahman shuffled over cautiously, trying not to disturb his historical musings. Leaning in, he whispered into Grandpa's ear like a secret agent passing classified information.

"Grandpa," Jahman began, his voice dripping with desperation, "I love History so much I could eat it for breakfast, lunch, and maybe even dinner. But tell me, do you have any dealings with Mr. Maths, or are you safe from him? Please, Grandpa, you've got to be my sanctuary!"

Grandpa paused, standing up straight and resting his weight on a wooden cane that looked older than the Industrial Revolution. He gave Jahman a long, piercing look from head to toe, his eyes twinkling. He gave the impression he knew something Jahman didn't.

"Mr. Runaway," he said, his voice deep and wise like the narrator of an epic documentary, "let me ask you this—without Mr. Maths, how would we calculate the time, day, and year when events happened? How would we measure centuries, decipher timelines, or chart the rise and fall of empires? History would be stratospherically boring without him!"

Jahman froze for the umpteenth time, mouth agape as if Napoleon himself had just handed him a defeat. "Grandpa," he stammered, "are you telling me that Mr. Maths is responsible for organising all of history? The dates, the years, the timelines—all of that is his doing?"

Grandpa History chuckled softly, stroking his long, imaginary beard for dramatic effect. "Of course, my boy. What do you think we use to calculate how long the Hundred Years' War lasted? Or how the Gregorian calendar came to be? Maths is the backbone of History!"

Jahman's heart sank like a cannonball into a muddy battlefield. So even the noble History, his beloved Grandpa, had ties to the sinister Mr. Maths. He sighed, looking down at the ground where historic footprints had been etched into the earth. "Even here," he muttered under his breath, "Maths has infiltrated."

Grandpa History, clearly amused by Jahman's existential crisis, patted him on the shoulder. "Cheer up, lad," he said with a wink. "At least you're not stuck calculating inflation during the Great Depression or figuring out Napoleon's battle logistics. That's when Maths really gets spicy!"

But his words didn't comfort Jahman. He trudged away from the battlefield, shaking his head and muttering, "Maths is not hot. Even in History, Maths is lurking. Where can I escape to now? Is there anywhere left?"

Catering

After Jahman's encounter with Grandpa History, he decided to seek refuge with Madam Chef, Catering. His dream was to become Gordon Ramsay one day, so he dashed to the kitchen and found Madam Chef competing on *MasterChef* on BBC One.

Madam Catering: Hello, Mr. Maths-Phobia! How are you?

Jahman: (Muttering) Why is everyone calling me Maths-Phobia? (Clearing his throat) Well, as you already know, I despise Mr. Maths. But I love to cook, and my dream is to be the next Gordon Ramsay. Can you help me achieve that?

Madam Catering: (Smiling; hands Jahman a piece of paper) This one's for you, Mr Gordon Ramsay, who is in training.

Ama is making Chilli Con Carne. Here is a list of ingredients to serve 6 people:

1.2kg mince meat

420g tomatoes

3 chillies

600g kidney beans

Ama wants to make enough Chilli Con Carne for 18 people. How much of each ingredient does she need?

Jahman: (Shocked) Madam Catering, is this not a direct proportion or ratio from Mr. Maths' lessons? Why are you subjecting me to numeracy? This is not catering! I thought catering was about gathering ingredients and just cooking them! (Becoming desperate) I think I need to go to Specsavers because I can't even see what's on this paper.

Design and Technology

After Jahman's catastrophic failure in front of Madam Chef, he stumbled upon Mr. Tesla, the Design and Technology master, leaning against his futuristic SUV—a sleek car equipped with a periscope and a 2050 registration plate.

Jahman: Hello, Mr. Tesla! I'm finally all yours. No one else wants to give me a safe haven. I'm ready to surrender to your wisdom because I genuinely love designing things. I want to design a dining table for my mother. Could you please help me?

Mr DT: Well, Mr. Runner, you've come to the right place. I have a proposition for you. Here's the plan:

Design Brief:

You're designing a rectangular tabletop for a school project in Design and Technology. The tabletop must be strong, lightweight, and made from a single sheet of plywood.

Specifications:

The tabletop's area must be 1.5 m². The length of the tabletop should be 1.5 times its width.

Tasks:

1. Calculate the dimensions (length and width) of the tabletop.

2. The plywood sheet costs £8.50 per square metre. Calculate the total cost of the plywood for the tabletop.

3. If the tabletop edges need to be sanded and the cost of sanding is £0.75 per metre, calculate the total sanding cost for the tabletop's perimeter.

Jahman stared at the brief, mystified. Then he inched closer to Mr. DT and muttered into his ear: "Mr. DT, you're embarrassing me. You know I despise Mr. Maths! How on earth do you expect me to calculate the dimensions of a tabletop, let alone the total cost of plywood or sanding?"

As he walked away, shaking his head, Jahman thought to himself: 'What a wonderful world.'

RE

After yet another crushing defeat in his war against Maths, Jahman decided to soothe his battered ego with a nostalgic trip down memory lane. Tottenham's epic 2022 victory over Arsenal in the top-four race seemed like the perfect distraction. But as he wandered near St. Paul's Cathedral, fate had other plans.

Emerging dramatically from the grand doors was none other than Mr. Preacher, the RE teacher, Bible in hand and looking every bit like a prophet descended from a Renaissance painting. Across the courtyard, leaning casually against a cherry-red Tesla, stood Mr. Hammer, the DT teacher, exuding his trademark 'cool guy' energy. The contrast couldn't have been more cinematic: the fire-and-brimstone preacher versus the tech-savvy innovator. Naturally, Jahman was drawn in.

As he approached, their voices carried toward him like an unscripted play. Mr. Preacher, in full sermon mode, gestured emphatically with his Bible, practically vibrating with divine conviction.

"You must stop designing gadgets and flashy cars, my son!" he thundered, pointing accusingly at Mr. Hammer. "Jesus Christ is coming soon, and the end of the world is upon us! Why waste time on inventions when Matthew 24 lays it all bare? Wars! Earthquakes! Technology is infiltrating every corner of life! Read the signs—they're everywhere!"

Mr. Hammer, typically unbothered by anything short of a design flaw, nodded solemnly as though the Tesla's bonnet had just absorbed the burden of humanity's sins.

Sensing his moment to shine, Jahman stepped forward with a flourish. "Mr. Preacher!" he declared. "I'm a believer! I follow all ten commandments. Please, make me a disciple of Jesus Christ!"

Mr. Preacher turned, fixing Jahman with a gaze so intense it could've melted the stained glass behind him. "Take your Bible," he commanded, "and open it to Matthew, chapter 14. In this chapter, Jesus feeds five thousand people with five loaves of bread and two fish. Now, tell me—how many basketfuls of leftovers did the disciples collect?"

Jahman blinked, his confidence crumbling. "Wait... since when did RE team up with maths?"

"Numbers," Mr. Preacher sighed, closing his Bible with the kind of finality that sends shivers down your spine, "are how we locate chapters and verses. Without numbers, the Word would be lost. Numbers are divine."

"But... I hate numbers," Jahman stammered.

With a sigh that seemed to echo off the cathedral walls, Mr. Preacher intoned, "Then you cannot be a disciple of Jesus Christ."

Panic set in. "But I really want to be a disciple!" Jahman begged.

Mr. Preacher's eyes narrowed as he delivered the ultimate bombshell: "Then you must embrace Numbers—and by extension, Mr. Maths. Numbers, my child, are the universal language of the entire world."

The realisation hit Jahman like a lightning bolt from the heavens. Maths wasn't confined to classrooms and textbooks. It was lurking everywhere. In sermons. In life. In the sacred act of feeding five thousand people with miraculous bread and fish. Horrified, he staggered backwards, his dreams of discipleship crumbling under the weight of equations.

"Nooo!" Jahman gasped, turning to flee. His only hope was Mr. Hammer, his saviour in the form of Tesla-driving practicality. But before he could beg for sanctuary, the world tilted. His vision blurred. And just as he was about to plead for mercy, everything went black.

Perhaps Jahman had fainted from the sheer existential terror of realising that Maths truly was inescapable. Or maybe it was divine intervention, sparing him from further humiliation. Either way, one thing was clear: his battle with Maths—and his journey of acceptance—was far from over.

Chapter 9:
From Coma to Clarity – Jahman's Maths Epiphany

Jahman blinked awake in a hospital bed at Northwick Park, his eyes struggling against the blinding ceiling lights like they owed him money. A nurse stood over him with a clipboard, smirking like she knew something he didn't.

"Well, well," she said, tapping her pen. "You've been out for a few weeks. But even in your coma, guess what you wouldn't shut up about?"

Jahman raised an eyebrow.

"Maths," she said. "You kept mumbling stuff like, 'Maths is hot. Numbers are life... Angles don't lie... The world is a giant equation.' You sounded like a motivational calculator."

Maths Is Not Hot

Jahman groaned, dragging the blanket over his face like it could protect him from the shame. "So now maths is haunting my dreams too? Brilliant."

As the machines beeped rhythmically around him, something began to click—slowly, like a buffering video. No matter how many subjects he fled to—Drama, History, Art—or how many fake nosebleeds he staged, maths kept turning up like that uninvited aunty who always brings stew but never leaves.

For most of his school life, Jahman had treated maths like it was the villain in a horror movie: always lurking, always ready to pounce with equations that made no sense. Algebra was a code only aliens understood, fractions were a scam, and geometry? Pure chaos with a ruler. But now, lying in a hospital bed with nothing but time and a dodgy vending machine in sight, he began to see things differently.

Maths Is Not Hot

Maybe—just maybe—maths wasn't trying to ruin his life. Maybe it had just been badly introduced, like a misunderstood side character in a telenovela.

"How do I even start?" he thought aloud. "Do I shake his hand? Send a text? Offer him some jollof rice with salmon or jerk chicken?"

And then it hit him: *"The Why Mummy Method"* (Anarfi-De-Khems, 2023)—a way of learning by always asking **why**. Why does it work like that? Why does x even need to be found? Why does this matter outside the exam hall?

The more he asked "why," the more maths started making actual sense.

Could it be that maths wasn't his enemy... just badly explained?

With a deep sigh and a twitch of his IV line, Jahman decided: maybe, just for a second—a munite, tops—he'd give maths a chance.

After all, it had chased him this far. Might as well see what all the fuss was about.

Why, Mummy? The Secret to Understanding Maths

Maths can feel like one big mystery sometimes, can't it? Despite the government's best efforts to "simplify the curriculum," people like Jahman are still out here acting like maths is written in ancient Egyptian hieroglyphs. So what's really going on? Why does it still feel so hard—and more importantly, how do you finally *get it*?

Meet Jahman. A regular student with an irregular relationship with maths. Sometimes, it clicks. Other times, it's like he's been handed a secret code meant for NASA scientists. One day in class, the teacher put an indices question on the board. Jahman stared at it like it had just insulted his ancestors.

"Why do we add the powers when multiplying indices?" he thought.

Everyone else was scribbling away, no questions asked. Jahman had two choices: pretend he got it... or ask the golden question— "Why?"

If you've ever wondered why we divide by two when finding the area of a triangle, or why a negative times a negative equals a positive, congrats—you're already halfway to becoming a maths genius. That curiosity? That's what we call conceptual understanding—it's all about knowing *why* things work, not just memorising rules like a human calculator.

So, how do you actually unlock the "why" behind all this maths stuff?

Simple: Be your three-year-old self again.

Remember that age when you questioned EVERYTHING? If you don't, just ask your mum—she's probably still traumatised.

Let's rewind:

Mum: Jahman, put on your jacket.

Jahman: Why, Mummy?

Mum: Because we're going shopping.

Jahman: Why, Mummy?

Mum: Because we need to buy food.

Jahman: Why, Mummy?

Mum: So you can eat.

Jahman: Why, Mummy?

Mum: So you can grow big and strong.

Jahman: Why, Mummy?

Mum: JAHMAN, PLEASE—CAN I BREATHE FOR ONE SECOND?!

Jahman: Why, Mummy?

Sure, tiny Jahman was annoying—but he was also *learning, exploring*, and trying to understand his world. And that relentless curiosity? That's exactly what you need for maths.

Next time you're stuck on a topic, don't just nod along. Be brave. Ask your teacher, *"Why, Sir?"* or *"Why, Miss?"* Dig deep. Be curious. Be annoying, even.

Because the truth is, the more "Why, Mummy?" questions you ask in maths, the clearer everything becomes.

So go on—unleash your inner Jahman. Let's dive in.

Why Asking "Why?" Matters in Maths

Meet Jahman. While the rest of the class silently obeys the maths gospel, he dares to question the sacred scrolls. 'But why does this even work?' he asks, shattering the silence.

Cue the groans. But Jahman's not trying to be difficult—he just wants to *understand*, not memorise.

One day in class, his teacher dropped this classic formula on the board:

Area of a trapezium = ½ × (a + b) × height

The rest of the class blinked, wrote it down, and carried on with their lives. But not Jahman. He squinted at the board like it owed him money. "Why do we divide by two? Where did this even come from?"

Instead of ignoring his confusion, Jahman leaned into it—and that's when everything changed.

His teacher broke it down with a visual trick:

1. Take the trapezium and make a copy.
2. Rotate the copy 180°.
3. Fit the two together like puzzle pieces so the slanted sides line up.

Boom—you've now got a parallelogram with a base of (a + b) and the same height.

And we *do* know how to find the area of a parallelogram:

Area = base × height

So:

Area = (a + b) × height

But remember, we only started with *one* trapezium, and now we've got *two*. So we halve it:

½ × (a + b) × height

Suddenly, Jahman didn't just remember the formula—he *understood* it.

And just like that, maths became less about cramming and more about connecting the dots.

That's the magic of conceptual understanding—it's like getting behind the scenes of a maths trick. Instead of trying to memorise a million formulas and panicking when you forget one, you understand *why* it works. You can rebuild it from scratch.

It's a maths superpower. You stop being a passive note-taker and start becoming a problem-solving ninja—spotting patterns, making connections, and figuring things out *even when you forget the rules*.

So next time something doesn't make sense, don't stay quiet.

Be like Jahman. Ask, "Why?"

Stay curious—and watch how maths goes from mysterious to *mastered*.

How Jahman Turned Maths into His Buddy

Jahman's relationship with maths? Let's just say... it was complicated. In his family, numbers were treated like cursed objects—feared, avoided, and definitely not discussed at the dinner table. As far as Jahman was concerned, maths had a personal vendetta against him.

The way it was taught? Straight-up sorcery. Teachers hurled formulas at him like magic spells, expecting students to chant them back with zero explanation.

Pythagoras' Theorem? Dark magic.

Quadratic equations? Ancient hieroglyphics.

It wasn't that maths was evil—it just made no sense. It felt like trying to solve a Rubik's Cube blindfolded, underwater... during an earthquake.

Then came Mr. Dee.

Cool, calm, and basically a Jedi Master of numbers, Mr. Dee didn't just *teach* maths—he *decoded* it. He turned lifeless formulas into real-life puzzles, transformed boring drills into lightbulb moments, and—best of all—he actually liked it when students asked questions. No dramatic sighs. No eye rolls. Just good vibes and solid explanations.

Jahman took that and ran with it.

He soaked up Mr. Dee's motivational maths pep talks.

He started using the **Why Mummy Method** in class (asking "why?" until the fog cleared).

He did all his homework—even when it felt like wrestling a calculator in the dark.

And he became a past paper ninja, mastering old exam questions like they were cheat codes to success.

Wanna know how he pulled that off? Let's break it down—one legendary step at a time.

Jahman vs Mr. Dee and the "Why, Mummy?" Method

Jahman wasn't the quiet, nodding-along type. Nah—he was the student who tilted his head, squinted at the board, and asked the question most were too shy to voice:

"But why, though?"

He wasn't being a smart aleck. He had just discovered a superpower: *curiosity*. Memorising steps without knowing *why* felt like learning dance moves with no music. He was done being a robot—he was ready to be a detective.

One day, Mr. Dee stood at the front of the class, full of energy.

"Today, we're finding the area of a triangle," he announced, scribbling the formula on the board:

Area = ½ × base × height

Most students blinked, copied, and mentally checked out.

Not Jahman.

"Wait, Sir… why do we even need to know this?"

Mr. Dee didn't flinch. "Good question. Say you're designing a flag, cutting a slice of pizza, or planning a triangular garden—you'd need to know how much space you're working with. That's what area tells us."

Jahman nodded slowly... but his hand shot back up.

"Okay, but *why* do we divide by two?"

The room tensed. Was this a challenge?

Mr. Dee grinned. "Excellent. Let's talk pizza."

"Now we're talking," Jahman perked up.

"Imagine a big rectangular pizza. You cut it diagonally from corner to corner—what do you get?"

"Two triangle slices!"

"Exactly. That diagonal cut splits the rectangle perfectly in half. So a triangle is literally half a rectangle with the same base and height. That's why we divide by 2."

"So triangles are undercover pizza slices?"

"Pretty much," Mr. Dee laughed. "Just don't try putting pepperoni on your homework."

Jahman wasn't done.

"Why do we use base and height?"

"The base is the triangle's bottom, and the height is how tall it stands from that base. It's like measuring how much room it takes up."

"Got it. So what's first?"

"Plug in the values. Base: 6cm. Height: 8cm."

"So... Area = ½ × 6 × 8"

"Exactly."

"Why multiply before dividing?"

"Another good 'why'! It's part of the order of operations—multiply first, then divide. Makes it easier."

"Okay, 6 × 8 = 48. Then 48 ÷ 2 = 24."

"Boom! Area = 24 cm². The little ² means we're measuring space—not just length."

Jahman grinned. "So if I design a giant triangle-shaped pizza, I'll know *exactly* how much cheese I need."

The class cracked up. Mr. Dee laughed too.

"Exactly! And now you're ready to take on any triangle mystery—one 'why' at a time."

Homework: Jahman's Plot Twist

Jahman's attitude toward homework did a full 180—like one of those wild soap opera twists where the villain turns out to be the long-lost twin. Gone were the days he saw it as some medieval torture device crafted by teachers to ruin his evenings.

He was done playing the victim.

"Homework isn't punishment," he declared, striking a superhero pose in front of the mirror.

"It's my training ground. My practice pitch. My three-pointer drill."

He thought about Muhammad Ali—the champ who once said:

"I hated every minute of training, but I said, 'Don't quit. Suffer now and live the rest of your life as a champion.'"

If Ali could push through brutal workouts, Jahman figured he could survive a few algebra questions without flopping to the floor in fake agony (...probably).

Besides, Cristiano Ronaldo and Lionel Messi didn't become football GOATs by bingeing TV and manifesting goals into existence. They trained. They practiced. They took ice baths—which, let's be honest, sounded way worse than a maths worksheet.

And Steph Curry? He didn't just wake up casually swishing 500 three-pointers. He put in the reps.

Turns out, science agrees. Regular homework really *does* help.

"Our study provides strong evidence that regular homework can significantly enhance student performance—especially when given 'little and often'." (Nathan McJames, lead author of a 2024 study from Maynooth University).

Even research says: greatness isn't crammed. It's built one small, sweaty effort at a time.

Jahman looked at his worksheet, pumped.

"If Curry can shoot 500 hoops, I can do ten algebra problems. Fair trade."

Even if he didn't know how to do them, the guessing days were over. No more scribbles. No more hoping for miracle marks. If he didn't get it, he'd ask a mate, search it up, or go straight back to the teacher for a proper breakdown.

From that moment, homework became his personal boot camp.

Every question? A free kick.

Every equation? A layup.

Every mistake? Just part of the drill.

"Homework isn't just busywork," Jahman told himself, pen in hand.

"It's how I train my brain to dunk on exams. "Game on.

Past Questions: Jahman's Secret Weapon

But Jahman didn't stop at homework—oh no. He went full GOAT mode, setting his sights on the holy grail of exam prep: past questions.

To him, these weren't just dusty old worksheets—they were game footage before a championship match.

"If Messi studies defenders to predict their moves, I can study past papers to outsmart the exam," he declared, with the swagger of someone who'd just unlocked the cheat codes to success.

And he was *right*. Jahman wasn't just stuffing random facts into his brain—he was training it. He learned to spot patterns, predict the curveballs, and move through questions like a seasoned exam ninja.

Not Just Hard Work—Smart Work

Jahman's strategy wasn't just about grinding—it was backed by science. Research (shout out to *Boaler, 2016*) shows that practising past questions boosts not just grades, but confidence. The more familiar you are with exam-style problems, the less likely your brain is to freeze on test day.

Jahman wasn't walking into the exam hall blindfolded, drenched in sweat, whispering last-minute prayers.

Nah. He'd already sparred with these questions on Tuesday nights with a bowl of jollof by his side.

"Bring it on," he smirked, flipping open his first big test. "I've seen tougher ones during revision."

Each question he cracked? A goal.

Every correct answer? A win.

And with every page, his confidence soared—proof that he hadn't just studied hard, he'd studied *smart*.

Even the National Council of Teachers of Mathematics (yes, the NCTM!) would've given Jahman a standing ovation. They say practising different types of problems sharpens adaptability.

But Jahman didn't need a research paper to tell him that—he'd already figured it out in real life.

The Art of Outsmarting the Examiner

Jahman treated past papers like treasure maps.

"Oh, they love throwing in this tricky algebra trap," he'd say, spotting patterns like a detective. "I see you, examiner. Not today."

He didn't waste time flexing on the easy stuff. He hunted the nightmare questions—the ones that made the class collectively groan.

"If I can wrestle with the tough ones now," he reasoned, "the actual exam will feel like a warm-up."

And when exam day finally rolled around?

While others flipped through textbooks like their lives depended on it, stress levels peaking at DEFCON 1, Jahman sat cool and collected. He had done the work. He'd studied the plays.

First question popped up.

Jahman grinned.

"This one again? Light work."

Past questions weren't just prep. They were power-ups.

A Self-Motivated Learner with a Passion for Problem Solving

Jahman wasn't just flicking through past questions like the average student on a revision mission — oh no. He was deep in the mathematical trenches, challenging himself like a number-slinging ninja. Curiosity didn't just kill the cat; in Jahman's case, it led him straight into the wild lands of AQA Level 2 Further Maths and Edexcel Level 3 Algebra, armed with nothing but sheer determination and a Casio calculator.

While most students were still getting their heads around basic trigonometry, Jahman was out here dancing with derivatives and flirting with functions. The Level 3 algebra gave him a backstage pass into the world of abstract thinking, while AQA Further Maths was the protein shake strengthening his calculus core. By the time Mr.

Dee even *mentioned* a new topic, Jahman had already pre-gamed it online, cross-checked it with three YouTube channels, and solved a problem set just for fun — because why not?

He wasn't just showing up to lessons anymore—he was showing up with 90% of the topic already tucked in his mental backpack like snacks for a hike. And that extra 10%? He wasn't wasting it. Jahman was diving into **NRICH**, battling puzzles on **UKMT**, and treating problem-solving like it was the Champions League of maths.

He was on fire.

And guess what? Jahman's obsession with problem solving wasn't just some nerdy phase—it's actually backed by research. As Pragati Sinha puts it:

"Problem-solving in math education encourages students to think critically and logically. It requires them to analyze a problem,

identify relevant information, and develop a solution using reasoning and evidence. These critical thinking skills are not only essential for math but also transferable to other subjects and real-life situations." (Pragati Sinha, *Mathematics Learning Link*, 2023).

So yeah—maths became his sidekick. His sparring partner. His slightly annoying but weirdly lovable roommate. And most shocking of all? He was having fun. Yes, fun… with maths.

At this point, Jahman was doing laps around the classroom helping his peers like some unofficial teaching assistant. Mr. Dee even started referring to him as "Mr. Jahman" during group tasks. Was he paid for his services? No. But did he act like a man who's billing Ofsted for every explanation he gave on completing the square? Absolutely.

Jahman didn't just learn maths — he *lived* it. And judging by his enthusiasm, mathematical talent, and willingness to lift others up with him, he's not just preparing to teach maths — he's about to make it cool.

Victory: From 2% to Grade 9

Jahman didn't just pass maths—he obliterated it. A Grade 9 never tasted so sweet

Why? Because he trained like a champion.

If Messi's out here stalking defenders like an Instagram crush...

If Steph Curry's shooting hoops like it's a video game level-up...

If Ronaldo's freezing his thighs for the sake of glory...

Then what's your excuse for skipping past questions before the big game?

Maths may not come with a trophy—but winning is winning. And Jahman just brought home the gold.

Even better? He broke the Asona family curse—the one that had haunted his bloodline for generations.

From zoning out in class, drowning in maths anxiety, struggling with ADHD, and scoring a soul-crushing **2%**, to acing a Grade 9?

Jahman flipped the script.

He's not just a student anymore.

He's a maths legend.

And if Jahman can break a generational curse—what's stopping you?

How Did Jahman Do It?

You're probably wondering:

Did he sell his soul to the Maths Gods?

Unlock a secret formula buried in an ancient scroll?

Get bitten by a radioactive calculator?

Nope. Jahman cracked the code the smart way.

He didn't just memorise formulas—he asked "WHY?" He went beyond the numbers and dug into the logic behind every concept. That's called conceptual understanding—and it's a game-changer.

He did his homework. For real. Even when it felt like mental gymnastics, Jahman showed up. And if he got stuck? He didn't fake it—he asked for help, instead of handing in scribbles and hoping for a miracle. He practiced like a champion.

Jahman didn't just *learn* maths—he went full beast mode.

Past papers? He devoured them like pre-workout snacks.

He tackled Nrich problems, battled UKMT challenges, and wrestled with Further Maths and Level 3 Algebra like he was prepping for the Maths Olympics... and aiming for gold. No spells. No secret hacks.

Just strategy, sweat, and a whole lot of swagger. And the best part?

If Jahman could do it...So. Can. You.

Maths: The Unexpected MVP of Life

So when Jahman raised his hand for the 37th time in a single lesson to ask, *"But WHY are we doing this?"* Mr. Dee didn't groan, roll his eyes, or hit him with the dreaded *"Just memorise it."*

Instead, he leaned in, grinned, and said, "Let me show you."

Maths Is Not Hot

And just like that, maths started feeling less like an evil overlord... and more like a buddy worth getting to know.

Algebra: The Detective's Toolkit

"Think of algebra like solving mysteries," Mr. Dee said. "It's about finding the missing piece of the puzzle—like being a detective, but with numbers. You know when you're saving up for those limited-edition sneakers and need to figure out how many weekends of chores it'll take? That's algebra. Architects use it to keep skyscrapers standing. Game developers use it to make characters jump, run, and respawn. It's the secret weapon behind everyday problem-solving—clever, flexible, and always ready when you need it."

Jahman raised an eyebrow. "So you're saying I'm basically Sherlock Holmes meets Spider-Man... but with equations?"

Mr. Dee grinned. "Exactly. Great power, great algebraic responsibility."

Jahman squinted. "So, algebra's like... Sherlock Holmes, but with x and y?"

"Exactly," Mr Dee said, still grinning.

Fractions: The Pizza Police

"Fractions are all about fairness," Mr. Dee continued. "Ever shared a pizza with your friends? Fractions make sure no one steals your slice. And when you're baking a cake and need to halve the recipe? Fractions save the day. They help you split bills at a restaurant without drama and scale up your smoothie recipe without flooding the blender."

Jahman nodded slowly. "Okay, fractions might not be so bad. Especially if it means no one gets more jollof than me."

Powers: The Secret to Going Viral

"Powers are about growth—exponential growth," Mr. Dee explained. "Imagine you post a TikTok, and each person who watches it shares it with three friends. That's exponential growth. Before you know it, your video's viral, all thanks to powers. They're also what helps scientists calculate how fast bacteria spread—or how quickly your phone battery drains when you're on it all day. Even compound interest in your savings account? That's powers doing their thing."

Jahman's jaw dropped. "Wait, so powers are like... the maths behind TikTok fame?"

"That's right!" Mr. Dee replied with a grin.

Geometry: The Architect's Best Friend

"And geometry," Mr Dee said, drawing a triangle, "is the art of shapes and spaces. Footballers use it to calculate the perfect angle for a shot. Architects use it to design bridges and buildings. Even game designers use it to create those cool 3D graphics you love. Geometry is everywhere—it's what makes the world work."

Jahman blinked. "So geometry's like... the designer of the universe?"

"Now you're getting it!"

For the first time, Jahman didn't feel like maths was a foreign language. It wasn't about memorising formulas; it was about understanding why they mattered. And once he understood the why, the how became so much easier.

Maths: The Sneaky Genius Behind Everything

After Jahman started loving, understanding and becoming maths best friend, he also started noticing that maths wasn't confined to his school desk—it was *everywhere.*

'Everywhere?' he thought, skeptically. 'Nah, bruv. maths can't be running my life like that.'

Spoiler alert: it was. Maths is like that cousin who crashes every family gathering—always there, always judging, and secretly running the show.

Here's how maths was hiding in plain sight all along:

TikTok: Maths, But Make It Trendy

Ever wonder how TikTok decides which video to show you next? That's not magic; that's *maths*! Algorithms analyse your likes, comments, and watch time faster than you can say "For You Page." They predict what you'll binge next, turning numbers into your personal hype squad.

And those perfectly timed viral videos? They're built on fractions of a second. When you sync your moves to a beat, you're basically performing a live maths lesson on rhythm and timing. Want to nail that transition? Maths is doing the heavy lifting, one frame at a time.

Instagram: Maths Wears the Crown

Filters, hashtags, and engagement stats—Instagram is powered by maths, wearing a stylish beret.

Take the perfect selfie, for instance. It's all about symmetry and proportions, aka geometry's moment to shine. Ever heard of the golden ratio? It's the secret sauce behind those aesthetic grid layouts influencers love.

And when your post goes viral? Maths strikes again. Engagement metrics—likes, shares, and comments—are all calculated in ratios and percentages. Your 100 likes on a post with 50 followers? That's a 200% engagement rate. This means that, on average, each of your followers interacted with your post twice—or that people outside your follower list also engaged with your content. It's an insanely high engagement rate, which suggests your post either went viral or got a lot of attention beyond your usual audience. Maths just made you the Beyoncé of your feed.

Snapchat: Maths in Disguise

Snapchat may seem like all fun and dog-ear filters, but behind every selfie is a ton of maths. Facial recognition technology maps your face using points and lines (hello, geometry), then adjusts filters to fit your features.

Even those streaks you obsess over? Pure maths. Counting, tracking metrics, and a sprinkle of gamification keep you hooked. Maths isn't just behind Snapchat—it's running the whole operation, one rainbow-puke filter at a time.

Uber Drivers: Maths With a Steering Wheel

You think your Uber driver is just following the GPS? Nah, they're live-action mathematicians. Every decision they make—whether to take the highway or cut through side streets—is a real-time equation balancing speed, distance, and time.

That surge pricing you complain about? It's economics and percentages at work. Route optimisation, fuel efficiency, and earnings per trip? All powered by maths. The next time you're in an Uber, remember: you're basically sitting in a mobile maths lab.

Footballers: The Geometrical Geniuses of the Pitch

Football? Jahman thought it was all about raw talent, instinct, and the occasional lucky deflection. Turns out, footballers are low-key mathematicians in disguise. Every time they make a pass, they're secretly calculating angles like a human protractor. When they shoot, they're factoring in velocity, trajectory, and spin—basically pulling off physics experiments in real-time.

Free kicks? Oh, that's advanced maths. It's all about nailing the perfect bend with a mix of angles, speed, and precision. Goalkeepers?

They're out there predicting where the ball will land based on maths, not magic, while strikers tweak their shots to exploit gaps in the defense. And let's not forget team strategies—those are driven by stats, performance metrics, and more graphs than a maths textbook.

The football pitch? It's not just grass and lines; it's a massive geometry lesson in disguise. Forget VAR—maths is the real referee out there, silently calling the shots.

Jahman's Final Word: Make Maths Your Bestie

As Jahman reflects on his journey so far, he leans back in his chair with a thoughtful expression. "You know," he says, grinning, "I used to think I was the only one out here battling maths like it was a dragon I had to slay. But then I came across a little nugget of wisdom from someone who's basically the OG of maths legends—Albert Einstein. And let me tell you, this quote hit me like a lightning bolt:

"Do not worry about your difficulties in mathematics. I can assure you mine are still greater" (Albert Einstein).

He laughs, shaking his head. "Wait, so the guy who unlocked the secrets of the universe had *difficulties* with maths? I'm not gonna lie, that's kinda comforting. I mean, if Einstein himself was scratching his head over equations and still managed to become the most famous mathematician to ever live, then maybe there's hope for the rest of us. Right?"

Jahman shrugs with a wink. "So yeah, maths might still throw curveballs at me. But if Einstein could stumble and still go on to change the world, then who am I to complain? We all have our struggles, but it's how we rise above them that matters. And trust me, if Einstein can do it, so can we."

He smiles at his readers. "So don't let a little difficulty in maths hold you back. If the man who made $E=mc^2$ had a rough patch with his sums, then we've all got a shot at greatness. Now, go out there, grab those numbers, and turn them into your secret weapon. Who knows? You might just be the next Einstein... minus the crazy hair, of course."

So, stop running away from maths and start dancing to its beat. Who knows? You might just find yourself saying what Jahman never thought he'd admit: "Maths is... kinda awesome."

Jahman's Heartfelt Letter to Maths

Dear Maths,

Let's be honest—you and I didn't exactly hit it off in the beginning. If anything, we were sworn enemies. I thought you were out to ruin my life. Fractions? They made me question my entire existence. Algebra? That felt like deciphering hieroglyphics in an escape room with no exit. And geometry? Don't even get me started—those triangles were more cryptic than my aunty's secret jollof rice recipe.

You made me cry over homework, sweat through exams, and lose sleep over word problems that sounded like riddles from a sadistic troll. I even declared, with all the drama of a soap opera villain, "I'll NEVER need this in real life!" Oh, the irony.

But here's the plot twist, Maths—you're not the bad guy I made you out to be. You're not just a random subject designed to torture students. No, you're the ultimate life hack. Somewhere along the way, I started seeing you differently.

Now, I actually enjoy spending time with you. I even dream about you sometimes (weird, right?). I can't wait to get to school and learn more about your real-life magic. Turns out, you've been working behind the scenes all along, like a quiet genius making everything function while I ignored your brilliance.

You've been helping me nail the perfect jollof rice ratio, calculate discounts on sneakers, and even understand how footballers pull off those jaw-dropping free kicks. You've made baking cakes foolproof, saving money doable, and mortgages... well, less terrifying than they could've been.

You're not just numbers and formulas; you're the Beyoncé of the universe—the one running the whole show while everyone else is too busy vibing to notice.

So here's the truth: I'm sorry. I'm sorry for running away from you, for blaming you every time I got the wrong answer, and for thinking you were out to get me. You're not the villain in my story—you're the hero I didn't know I needed. The Robin to my Batman. The Samwise to my Frodo.

Thank you for sticking with me, even when I wanted nothing to do with you. You've turned out to be kind of brilliant, and I'm lucky to have you on my team.

Sincerely,

Jahman

P.S. I still don't love algebra, but I'm working on it. Don't push your luck.

BIBLIOGRAPHY

Anarfi-De-Khems, B. Teaching and Learning Mathematics for Understanding, submitted as coursework for MEMA702, University of Plymouth, January, 2023.

Boaler, J. (2015). *The elephant in the classroom: Helping children learn and love maths.* Souvenir Press.

Boaler, J. (2016). Mathematical Mindsets: Unleashing Students' Potential through Creative Math, Inspiring Messages, and Innovative Teaching.

Fernandez, C., & Yoshida, M. (2004). *Lesson Study: A Japanese Approach to Improving Mathematics Teaching and Learning.* Mahwah, NJ: Lawrence Erlbaum Associates.

Ma, L. (1999). *Knowing and Teaching Elementary Mathematics: Teachers' Understanding of Fundamental Mathematics in China and the United States.* Mahwah, NJ: Lawrence Erlbaum Associates.

McJames, N., Parnell, A., & O'Shea, A. (2024). *Little and often: Causal inference machine learning demonstrates the benefits of homework for improving achievement in mathematics and science*. Learning and Instruction. https://doi.org/10.1016/j.learninstruc.2024.101968

Ministry of Education, Singapore. (2012). *Mathematics Syllabus: Primary One to Six.* Retrieved from MOE Singapore

Ministry of Education and Research of Estonia. (2020). *Digital education in Estonia: Innovative learning for the 21st century.* Ministry of Education and Research of Estonia. https://www.hm.ee/en/activities/digital-education

Organisation for Economic Co-operation and Development (OECD). (2020). *Education Policy Outlook: Estonia.* OECD Publishing. https://doi.org/10.1787/9789264282013-en

OECD (2023), PISA 2022 Results (Volume I): The State of Learning and Equity in Education, PISA, OECD Publishing, Paris, https://doi.org/10.1787/53f23881-en.

Organisation for Economic Co-operation and Development (OECD). (2019). *PISA 2018 results (Volume I): What students know and can do.* OECD Publishing. https://doi.org/10.1787/5f07c754-en

Sahlberg, P. (2016). *Finnish lessons 2.0: What can the world learn from educational change in Finland?* Teachers College Press.

Sahlberg, P. (2015). *The Finnish way: Achieving equity and excellence in education.* Corwin Press.

Schleicher, A. (2019). *World Class: How to Build a 21st-Century School System.* OECD Publishing.

Sinha, P. (2023, March 13). *The Importance of Problem-Solving in Mathematics Education.* Mathematics Learning Link. Retrieved from https://mathematicslearninglink.com/2023/03/the-importance-of-problem-solving-in-mathematics-education/

www.ingramcontent.com/pod-product-compliance
Lightning Source LLC
Chambersburg PA
CBHW042043280426
43661CB00093B/985